THE HARD TRUTH!
STOPPING ALCOHOL!

Christopher J. Najera
The Hard Truth! Stopping Alcohol!

ISBN 979-8-89691-793-9

THE HARD TRUTH! STOPPING ALCOHOL!

LIVING ALCOHOL-FREE ON AN INTOXICATED EARTH

CHRISTOPHER J. NAJERA

CONTENTS

INTRODUCTION

One of the main reasons that ignited this book was wanting to help as many people as I possibly could from the flames of Alcohol. Also, I wanted to make sure that everything I was researching and discovering in the 2 years it took to stop drinking was going to be permanent and in writing for those seeking relief and understanding. You will read a lot about what I discovered and what you can expect when you stop. With a lot of prayers to my higher power (which will come in a later chapter) to give me wisdom and knowledge so I can help as many people as possible for years to come.

The premise of this book is to explore and uncover the problems associated with alcohol and its dependency. The book was designed to be read in two forms: from start to finish, or you can jump into a chapter that calls out to you. I recommend looking over the chapters and seeing if there is one that you want to read first. If you want to jump onto the 30-Day Road map you can start today on your alcohol-free journey in chapter 9. In the book you will find repetition in some of the chapters.

This is for those that want to jump to a chapter and learn what attracts you. I wanted to keep the core ideas of the book flowing out of each chapter.

I also added as much information on what the alcohol companies never expose about their products and how it is affecting millions who consume alcohol on a regular basis. The numbers are staggering and alarming when they are broken down by actual numbers and populations.

I dive into alcohol abuse and use, and the effects that no one ever talks about. You will also find every resource and guide to giving alcohol a true evaluation in your life, and if it really makes sense for what it's worth. I struggled for many years, not really understanding the repercussions of alcohol use. There are things that everyone's family needs to talk about, so you won't become a victim of the alcohol trap. Maybe you are in its trap and don't even know it.

This book is a resource that all families should start talking about at their dinner tables, especially if alcohol is consumed on a regular basis. Today alcohol is socially acceptable with every occasion, yet it destroys so many lives every year. I needed help at the end of my drinking days and could never find it. So, I wanted to create an all-in-one book that had every resource to help anyone trying to break the vicious cycle of alcohol. Or, if you're even a light weekend drinker that turns to alcohol on weekends regularly, this book can help you as well. Maybe you also got caught with a DWI and want to break down what role alcohol really plays in your life. This will help you!

In Chapter 9, I created a 30-day road map to follow and break free from habitual drinking. The only way this chapter of the book works is by taking it seriously and giving it a 30-day solid break. You need to create a paradigm shift in your thoughts, a new kind of thinking with courage and emotion. At the end you will have a different perspective and can evaluate what its role plays in your life.

I also don't intend to give a lot of fluff to make this book a 250-page novel, but to give you what I found on my journey to sobriety in the first two years I stopped drinking. It really makes this reading an all-in-one self-help guide to stopping Alcohol.

When it's time to escape the shackles of the booze, you will know, but sometimes it can be too late. This comes from a hard-working individual who got trapped with alcohol and its evil chains that almost destroyed me and my life. Time and time again, you will see that alcohol does this to hard-working individuals or individuals that don't see it as a problem. The mind and body have adapted, and the real problems lurk to exist.

I include all the thoughts and research I discovered during my two-year recovery from alcoholism. If you're looking to stop, you have come to the right place. What I learned in sobriety is when you stop, you find a new person—you're someone completely new, and you will be working to try to find your own Identity. You will be taking back the person you were supposed to be in the first place, before the alcohol disrupted your life.

I started writing this book in my sixth month of no-booze, going into my seventh month. It wasn't until I first said "enough," seeing all the damage it was causing me and the people it harmed around me. It was at that moment in time that made me want to stop completely. They say the threshold of pain needs to be greater than the reward to overcome life changing results. This goes with stopping alcohol, some hit rock bottom and others have health issues, while some just get sick and tired of being sick and tired.

It was also when I was in an outpatient facility, talking to people who were waiting for liver transplants. I witnessed their struggles. We had conversations when they were wondering if the liver they were to receive would agree with their body, and how long they had to live. They were placed on several medications they had to take just to be alive.

See, the alcohol will blind us to think that It's okay to keep going, when It's not. You will end up in the hospital, jail, or an early grave.

If it wasn't for the help of my fiancé, Jaymie, who was already sober for six months and prayed for me daily, I truly believe I wouldn't have stopped. Her prayers worked. She went through a lot of the changes, the same aches and pains that I went through. It was like she paved the way, and if it wasn't for her, I would have probably been six feet under. I am forever grateful for her always believing in me.

For any person that reads this book, if you have a drinking problem you will have to do whatever it takes for you and nobody else. One day at a time, and don't over-think it. If you keep struggling, stopping and starting again, you may need some medication to balance the chemistry in the brain. That is because alcohol has hijacked the dopamine and serotonin areas of the brain, which plays an important role in the decision-making areas of the brain. And you are already in the trap that alcohol gets us in.

You can work to see a mental health provider that deals with addiction. It can be LCDC (Licensed Chemical

Dependency Counselor), an outpatient facility, or counselors that know addiction and can help you.

You will see that everybody's journey is unique and different. It's our journey and is special to us. It's not a hypnotic audio tape or an expensive recovery program. It's "THE HARD TRUTH" Stopping Alcohol. That's it! Dedication and willpower to really want to change and stick to it. Take the 30-Day break from alcohol and see what your relationship really is with it. Learn where you stand with it and become aware of what it plays in your life. If it's time to stop, you have found the right place to start! This is how my journey began.

1

HOW MY JOURNEY BEGAN WITH ALCOHOL AND IT'S EVIL TRAP

I wanted to start this chapter with a quote from Brandon Lee, Bruce Lee's son:

"Immortality is to live your life doing good things and leaving your mark behind."

I hope this mark will help many people for years to come.

This short chapter is to give a basis of how I became addicted to alcohol and couldn't stop.

Growing up in a border town, we had a lot of access to alcohol. Juarez, Mexico was part of our city and within walking distance. If you wanted to cross the border, it was just a walk over a bridge, and you were in another country. You could create a fake ID and go into any bar at 15 or 16 years of age. This area was known as "the strip," consisting of nightlife, clubs and bars—plenty of places to drink.

Being young and curious kids, we would go, mingle, and get intoxicated. It didn't help being part of the Hispanic culture where alcohol is a staple in almost every activity. While my mom was Irish, Indian and English, my father was Hispanic, last name Najera, which has roots in Spain. From what I've been told, our family has origins in Aguascalientes, Mexico. I never really got into the genealogy of it all, but I wanted to give a little background on who is writing this book—especially if you're reading this from somewhere In the United States or the Midwest and not from El Paso or our Region.

My alcohol consumption started in the late '80s to early '90s. It began on the strip, with all the thriving bars—most likely tied to the cartel, though we didn't know it at the time. I was the younger sibling in a group of teenage partygoers. Being the youngest among my brother and his friends, I thought it would be fun to check it out. With no hesitation, I followed them to Juarez.

I was hesitant for my first time drinking there, but I went with the flow. I think after three or four beers, I didn't remember the rest. I just know I made it home and couldn't believe I had actually been out with a group of older guys. They looked out for me—but little did they know I had become a drinking monster with the booze.

ABCO—Alcoholic Beverage Consuming Organization—was the name of the drinking crew, throwing parties for different high schools in the area. I remember nights when friends would take up to 15 tequila shots. Keep in mind—we were 16 or 17 at the time. The main objective was to find a house where parents were out of town and older brothers or sisters would buy us the kegs. This is nothing to be proud of, but it happened, and it's how the problems all started for me.

These parties were money-makers: pay 8 bucks to get in and drink as many beers as you wanted. We had multiple kegs. Cars would fill the streets—300 teenagers or more at a time. There was also marijuana in the mix, and whispers of other drugs. Being young and dumb, of course there were those who would try it. It's a border town; there were ways to find it if you wanted it. I'll just leave it at that. Thank goodness for the El Paso Law Enforcement and DWI Task Force that does good for our city today.

It was in those early days that my weekly battle with alcohol began. I was an athlete, growing up—playing soccer, skiing, snowboarding and skateboarding. But we always had access to alcohol, and it was readily available.

Going through my twenties, I never realized what was happening. I went through the motions. Bar owners didn't care what they were doing so long as they made their money—and that's still true today. It's sad how bars overserve and destroy lives. To me, it's all part of the plan. Alcohol and alcohol companies are not our friends. It truly is an evil poison when you break it down.

Alcohol creates a delusion—it tricks you into believing you like it, only for you to feel like death hours later. There are so many times I don't know how I survived the hangovers. I think it was by the grace of God, and maybe the green tea I drank daily, or the milk thistle and vitamins I took—that kept me alive. I still tell myself I'm lucky to be alive.

The delusion is alcohol makes you believe you want it, or that you need it. You think it helps you. But really, it just causes problems again and again. It's like a shady salesman promising the moon and stars, only to sell you a fake gold chain that looked good in the package.

The work of alcohol is simple: to steal, kill and destroy. It's a potion designed to take over and convince us it's okay—that it's not hurting us. But it is. It's like cutting away at a tree until it eventually falls to its death. Given enough time, with regular use, alcohol will consume your life completely. Each drink makes it worse. It becomes more addictive—mentally and physically. The more you drink on a regular basis, the more your mind believes you need it to survive. Like water or food, your mind and body will crave and think that it wants or needs it.

Alcohol companies know exactly what they're doing. They've created the perfect concoction to keep consumers coming back—and to make their billions. For reference: Anheuser-Busch made $59 billion in revenue worldwide in 2023.

There's no real warning on their labels. The ads just say, "Drink responsibly"—but that rarely happens for those who consume it regularly. When you're on the outside looking in, you begin to see the truth. Is this really about a good time, or is it a plot to take everything from you while you're still healthy enough to keep drinking?

Alcohol will take away everything that matters in your life and in the end, it can take away your existence. It takes friendships, breaks families, steals your mind, your money—and most importantly, your identity.

Below are the real signs to watch for when it's starting to slowly destroy your life.

Signs that you are in trouble with alcohol:

- When you tell yourself you will have one drink, but it turns into six, eight, or more.
- When you wake up and immediately check your bank account to see how much you spent.
- When you lose your keys or wallet after a night (or day) of drinking.
- When you say, "I only drink on weekends," or "I only drink beer or wine."
- When you say, "I need a drink after this stressful day or week." (Once this happens, you have already started turning to alcohol for relief. You have fallen into the trap of alcohol addiction.)
- When you say, "It's not that bad. I won't get addicted—I can stop anytime." (Yeah, right, for a little while, until your mind craves it.)
- Received a DWI or multiple DWI's.

The best ones I have heard are: "No man, I don't drink that much." or "I drink only beer." When you're drinking for four or five nights out of the week you are in the alcohol trap seeking the high or euphoria it gives you.

There is no in-between with alcohol. Either you consume it or you don't. A small percentage of the population can say, "I'll have one," and then go six months or a year without another drink. But for many, it becomes a weekly—or even daily—habit. Eventually, you can become dependent.

We consume it because we think it helps us relax. But, in reality, it creates more stress and more problems. Alcohol releases cortisol—a stress hormone—so whatever stress you had before drinking, it only creates more stress to your mind and body. This is where the real problem begins. Alcohol sabotages our mind, body, and soul. This leads into the next chapter: The Hijack.

2

THE HIJACK: WHAT THE ALCOHOLIC COMPANIES NEVER EXPOSE.

MENTAL HEALTH CAN BE THE KEY TO BREAKING THE ALCOHOLISM CHAINS.

When we think of a hijack, we imagine some deranged group of people—like those who jumped on a plane and destroyed the World Trade Centers. Unfortunately, that instance resembles alcohol and the brain.

The addiction process starts in the mesolimbic dopamine system, the dorsal striatum, and the ventral striatum—areas of the brain associated with the reward pathways. Alcohol gives a sense of reward and imprints this in the brain's synaptic cleft, associating it with good times and chemical adaptations. The synaptic cleft is the gap between neurons where an electrical signal is converted into a chemical signal.

The brain is a sea of chemicals, and the more you alter this balance, the more you become hijacked. With ongoing, continuous drinking, your mind becomes reprogrammed—and you're pretty much hooked. Alcohol hijacks your dopamine and serotonin receptors, changing them for the rest of your life.

If you had any predisposition to alcohol, the first time you consumed it, your mind and body likely felt like a new person, confident, powerful, relaxed, like your stress had just left the building. That's exactly what it was intended to do.

For me, I snuck a beer from an ice chest at a young age and realized I really liked this stuff. Little did I know it would haunt me and cause the most traumatic and painful times of my life.

Don't get me wrong—some people don't feel that connection I am describing. But when you're predisposed—and your parents consumed alcohol—you have a probability of becoming a victim of heavy drinking. For some, once you take those first few sips it's over. You're now on the ride of a lifetime—until you stop, or you can't stop, and you need to, or it stops you. Now I will dive into the details of what is really going on, and what no one talks about: The Hard Truth.

I am going to dive into some numbers to show the role alcohol plays around the world. We are living on an intoxicated earth. In 2022, the population was 7.8 billion people, and out of those, 2 billion consumed alcohol on a regular basis. With that said, we have established that alcohol hijacks the brain in multiple ways. The euphoria that ethanol supplies is a craving that keeps you going back for more. When you have drank continuously for years alcohol then has become a need. Now you are fully hijacked!

Remember being a kid, and asking an older sibling or someone taller to swing you around for the fun of playing? For some of us we felt euphoria from that experience. That's the same area of the brain that alcohol affects. It keeps you coming back for more, saying, "Do it again."

Over time it reprograms the pathways and your thought

processes. It tricks you into thinking that everything will be okay, that the hangovers are not that bad. Alcohol will control you until you decide to quit, or you need to quit but indefinitely can't.

If you don't quit, you will live a miserable life, struggling and feeling like crap every weekend until you get sick and tired of it. The older you get, the more you realize this is no way to live—not to mention the people around you that you are affecting from drinking. It's a choice and it's up to the beholder.

When you choose recovery, it's about finding the best life we were meant to live. Being alive means wanting to live and make it a good life without the suffering that alcohol can cause you. You fight the good fight to find any way to get out, whatever it takes.

I will say this more than once: you need to start creating anger toward all the things alcohol took from you without you even realizing it. To help you stop, you need to feel some anger. It's a way to help you stop and get past those cravings.

If a friend stole from you and you thought they were your friend, would you still talk to them or keep them in your life? No! You'd develop resentment toward them. In the same way, you need to start developing that same hate toward the poison. It was never your friend to begin with. Once you understand that, you can start to stop the madness it has caused. It's either this—or live a miserable life of suffering horribly in the end with liver disease, kidney disease, or on dialysis three times a week just to stay alive. When the alcohol has reprogrammed your mind, it will take effort to slow down and stop.

Below is the breakdown of the addiction process:

Here's how alcohol addiction works on a neurological level:

1. **Dopamine Release:**
   - Ethanol stimulates the release of dopamine in the brain's reward center, the nucleus accumbens. Dopamine is a neurotransmitter associated with pleasure and reward. The surge in dopamine creates feelings of euphoria and reinforces the desire to repeat the behavior that led to its release.

2. **Reward Pathways:**
   - The brain's reward pathways are crucial in reinforcing behaviors that are essential for survival, such as eating and social interactions. Alcohol consumption hijacks these pathways, leading to a sense of reward and pleasure that the brain interprets as positive.

3. **Tolerance:**
   - With continued alcohol use, the brain adapts to the increased dopamine levels by reducing its own natural production of the neurotransmitter. This leads to tolerance, where individuals may need to consume more alcohol to achieve the same pleasurable effects. Causing more destruction to your physical being.

4. **Dependency:**
   - Chronic alcohol consumption can result in physical and psychological dependence. The brain adapts to the presence of alcohol and starts to function differently in its absence.

Withdrawal symptoms, such as anxiety, irritability, and cravings, can occur when an individual tries to quit or cut down on alcohol use.

5. **Neuroadaptation:**
   - Long-term exposure to alcohol induces neuroadaptations, altering the function of various neurotransmitter systems. This can lead to changes in mood, cognition, and behavior, contributing to the cycle of addiction.

6. **Compulsion and Loss of Control:**
   - Over time, the compulsion to seek and consume alcohol can become overwhelming, and individuals may find it challenging to control their drinking despite negative consequences. This is all due to the highjack and neurotransmitters that have been destroyed and or taken over.

It's important to note that genetic factors, environmental influences, and individual susceptibility also play roles in the development of alcohol addiction. Some people may be more predisposed to alcohol dependence due to genetic factors that affect their brain chemistry and response to alcohol.

The prevalence of alcohol dependence—or alcoholism—varies widely across different populations and regions. According to the World Health Organization (WHO), alcohol dependence affected approximately 240 million people world-wide in 2022. However, this number can fluctuate over time due to shifts in cultural norms, access to treatment, and awareness.

And let's be honest, this is just what gets reported. The real number is likely much higher and continues to rise every year. So, we are living on an alcohol-intoxicated Earth.

Here are the alcohol dependence factors:

- Genetic predisposition
- Environmental influences
- Mental health issues
- Socioeconomic status

Not every individual who drinks will develop dependence or addiction—but the risk is real, and it varies significantly from person to person.

Here are some statistics that really hit hard:

1.35 million people die each year due to road traffic accidents. However, it's important to note that not all of them are related to alcohol. Of these, 20 to 30% are associated with alcohol consumption. That equals approximately 270,000 to 405,000 deaths every year—globally—caused by accidents involving alcohol as a contributing factor. That's enough to wipe out an entire city. To give that number some perspective, here are a few examples of cities with populations with this amount of people:

1. Pittsburgh, Pennsylvania: Pittsburgh had an estimated population of around 301,000 as of 2020.
2. St. Louis, Missouri: St. Louis had an estimated population of around 301,000 as of 2020.
3. Cincinnati, Ohio: Cincinnati had an estimated population of around 303,000 as of 2020.

4. Newark, New Jersey: Newark had an estimated population of around 314,000 as of 2020.
5. Orlando, Florida: Orlando had an estimated population of around 295,000 as of 2020.

Please note that population estimates can vary from year to year, and these figures are approximate—according to ChatGPT 3.5.

This is just to show how devastating it can be to live on a planet that consumes alcohol regularly—and the number of people who die each year due to alcohol-related accidents.

In addition, here are some alarming facts that alcohol distribution companies don't want you to know. To put things into perspective:

The number of deaths attributed to alcohol-related illnesses can vary depending on factors such as geographic location, population demographics, and reporting methods. Globally, alcohol contributes to a significant burden of disease and mortality. According to the World Health Organization (WHO), alcohol is estimated to be responsible for approximately **3 million deaths** each year worldwide.

Here are some key points related to alcohol-related deaths:

1. **Direct Causes:** Alcohol can directly contribute to various health conditions that increase mortality rates, including liver disease (such as cirrhosis), cardiovascular diseases, cancers (such as liver

cancer), neurological disorders, and accidents or injuries resulting from alcohol intoxication.

2. **Indirect Causes:** In addition to direct health effects, alcohol misuse can also contribute indirectly to mortality through factors such as impaired judgment leading to risky behaviors (e.g., driving under the influence), violence, and social consequences such as relationship problems and unemployment.

3. **Underreporting:** It's important to note that the actual number of alcohol-related deaths may be underestimated due to challenges in accurately attributing deaths to alcohol, especially in cases where alcohol-related conditions contribute to or exacerbate other health issues.

To put this into perspective—alcohol-related tragedies can wipe out an entire city every single year. Again, according to the World Health Organization, 3 million people die annually due to alcohol-related causes.

Just think about that. Alcohol has the power to wipe out the equivalent of an entire city each year! Below are examples of cities with populations of 3 million or more—based on world-wide statistics of alcohol-related deaths and their total numbers: A Hard Truth that no one ever talks about!

1. Los Angeles Metropolitan Area: Los Angeles is the second-largest city in the United States, with a population of over 4 million people. The Los Angeles metropolitan area, which includes surrounding cities and counties in Southern

California, has a population of over 13 million people.

2. Chicago Metropolitan Area: Chicago is the third-largest city in the United States, with a population of over 2.7 million people. The Chicago metropolitan area, which includes the city and its suburbs in Illinois, Indiana, and Wisconsin, has a population of over 9 million people.

3. Dallas-Fort Worth Metropolitan Area: Dallas and Fort Worth are major cities in Texas, with populations of over 1.3 million and 0.9 million people, respectively. The Dallas-Fort Worth metropolitan area, also known as the DFW Metroplex, has a population exceeding 7 million people.

4. Houston Metropolitan Area: Houston is the largest city in Texas, with a population of over 2.3 million people. The Houston metropolitan area, which includes the city and its suburbs in Southeast Texas, has a population of over 7 million people.

These are just a few examples of metropolitan areas in the United States with populations exceeding 3 million people. This is just to show the correlation and devastation alcohol does each year.

These numbers are alarming when it comes to the number of deaths alcohol can cause. The Hard Truth is that alcohol kills millions of people every year. I know I want to be here as long as I can. Now is the time to pray for anyone trapped by this evil potion and the takeover alcohol creates—often without people even realizing what is happening when they drink. In my early days of being sober, I asked people if they knew that alcohol killed this many people yearly. Not one person knew this statistic. Something that needs to get out to the masses.

I have had conversations with alcoholics, and it's very clear that they don't want to see or admit it is a problem. It's as if they are completely brainwashed and hypnotized by ethanol. They want to tell themselves they are okay, that they are cutting back, or that they can stop anytime— "It's not a big deal." But it could be already too late, and they don't even know it.

Not waking up the next morning or waking up to find you don't remember the night before—or worse, mixed it with other drugs and suffered a massive heart attack. It's selfish and unfair—not just to yourself, but to your family. It causes life-long pain and misery.

The crazy part about the hijack is that we don't realize it's happening—until one day something alarms us, but we don't listen to it, and we keep going further and further into the abyss. Also, alcohol will literally tell you that you don't have a problem. You start having thoughts like "I am fine", "It doesn't affect me as much anymore," or "I've got it under control." But not if you keep going back to it—week after week, month after month.

The cycle of alcohol is real. It starts as a want—that continues until your mind is altered and you keep going back— and turns into a need. The worst part is you don't even realize it. Meanwhile, alcohol companies continue putting money in their pockets. In

2024, Anheuser-Busch InBev (AB InBev) reported $59.77 billion in revenue, with a profit of $5.86 billion. They will never care, and people will keep spending their hard-earned money, fueling this industry that takes so many lives each year again and again.

The hidden truth is that the more you drink, the more problems begin to surface over time. When you're drinking regularly you don't see it as a problem. Alcohol is good at working to make you believe that it's not affecting you and your mental state. Stopping—before it gets worse is one of the most rewarding accomplishments you will make. When you stop, you will find yourself becoming more rational and more compassionate towards others. Not to mention the creative and empowering individual you can become. When I stopped, I had my mental battles—but my thoughts started to change, and I was learning new ways to process my thoughts. It was a slow process, and the sober magic happened at about one year off the sauce. You get the opportunity to truly live life. Alcohol destroys it—twice as fast. We don't even see that it is destroying us each time we consume.

Did you know the odds of being born are estimated to be 1 in 400,000,000,000,000? This is due to several factors that include: genetic combination, the chance of your parents meeting, and the number of sperm to egg ratios. The point is, you got this miraculous chance to see life and be alive, and you have been destroying it with alcohol.

I hope this makes sense. You can stop—with some hard work and willpower! The key is to commit to whatever it takes. If you're suffering from the damage of alcohol, there is a way out. Sobriety is the new way to live for many. It's safe to remember your mind can live without it. Also, it will function better without it. We were not born with an alcohol addiction, and it can be reversed.

I want to add this—if you've struggled like I did in the beginning, when trying to quit. You kept going back and didn't realize why, your mind is already in a state where you need medical help. And when I say medical help, I mean with medication. This will help stabilize your mind and correct the chemical imbalance.

In my darkest days, I would find myself on autopilot—driving to liquor stores, not even realizing what I was doing. It was like being a zombie, completely hypnotized. It wasn't until I talked to a mental health provider in a treatment setting that I realized my brain chemistry was completely out of balance—from the alcohol hijack. I needed medication to stabilize it. I found later in my recovery and talking to others that they also witnessed this behavior of autopilot drinking. Proving to me that alcohol addiction is real for many and I wasn't the only one that had witnessed this. Not realizing why, I was drinking, and I didn't even want to but did it anyway.

Getting medication was a game change for me—it helped me step away from the abyss. Stabilizing medications like Trazodone, Buspirone, and Wellbutrin helped tremendously. Some people take Naltrexone, which acts as an Antabuse for alcohol, and I have heard it was also a game changer.

I am not a doctor, and I don't recommend you use any of these. My mental health provider chose the right treatment for me based on the abuse and my history. You can work to get a mental health provider and get the help you need. Not all medications worked in the beginning for me. Some only gave me more cravings. But they switched them and found the key to unlock my recovery. It's best to be open and honest with your provider so they can figure out something that will work for you.

These medications helped stabilize the areas of my brain that were hijacked, my dopamine and serotonin transmitters. The best way I can describe it: I was able to land the plane and get grounded. For me, Wellbutrin and Buspirone took the craving away. Later I found that Buspirone effects became different, and I stopped taking it.

If you are struggling to stop, I recommend making an appointment and talking to a mental health provider to see what they can do to help you. Look for someone who deals with substance abuse, knows the addiction process and can work to help stabilize the mind. This is the real game-changer and can bring back the mind to be more stable.

I got the medication when I entered an outpatient program. I remember asking them how come nobody knows about this? This can help so many who can't stop and want to. They answered, "that's why these places exist, and they work if more would give it a try." It completely changed my life and got me on track.

One thing they told me was to dig deep and try to figure out why I drank so much. I started thinking a lot—Why was I drinking so much? What was alcohol doing for me? The answer was that it gave me the confidence to do the job I was in—the field I had chosen. It made my career in the ever-challenging and tough world of sales, it seemed to make things easier. I believed alcohol gave me the confidence to overcome my anxiety, but the more I consumed, the more I was in its trap.

It really wasn't helping my sales—it was hurting them. I recommend asking yourself, "Why do I drink so much?"

"What can I do to make the change I need to get sober"? This can help uncover the root cause of your struggle with alcohol. A mental health provider can assist you in finding the right medication and stabilize your mind.

Some may have a past they are trying to block out—memories they don't want to face. Medication can help with this. Maybe you have social anxiety, as I did and there is medication for that too. Another reason people drink and fall for the hijack is the belief that alcohol helps with your problems or relieves the stress of the week or day. The truth is it only creates more stress for both your mind and body. That's the smoke and mirrors that alcohol creates.

Long term use also destroys the white matter of the brain, the part primarily responsible for transmitting information between multiple regions of the brain. Alcohol deteriorates this, and over time, it can lead to Alzheimer's and dementia. As we age, these areas of the brain naturally decline, but alcohol accelerates this process. Having two drinks a day shrinks your brain as much as a decade of aging. The time may vary per individual but brings us closer to an older age than living without it.

Maybe you have had a difficult or abnormal life or childhood, and you drink to cover it up. It's better to face misfortune, have closure and move on from it. Drinking only masks the problem and never lets you completely have closure. Sometimes it takes some hard moments in reality to get to a better place from your past.

We need to realize that alcohol is not a solution to our problems. It might take the problem away temporarily, but it never goes away. Maybe you've lost a loved one or your family has fallen apart, and you've turned to the bottle for relief. This will only intensify those feelings and make you more depressed.

We've all heard that alcohol is a depressant and the truth is, it will only sink you deeper into the hole of depression the more you drink. Whatever your personal demons are, there are better ways to deal with them—and someone who can help you.

Get involved with a 12-step program like AA. Sometimes a counselor can also guide you. Alcoholics Anonymous is a fellowship that has helped millions recover and stop drinking. You can search online for a mental health provider in your area and find one that fits your needs.

3

THE DESTRUCTION
(ALCOHOLS HIDDEN AGENDA)

When talking about the destruction caused by alcohol, we think of the problems alcohol can cause us. We have all heard of them, and we can all talk about them. When you talk to someone deeply in alcohol addiction, they will not acknowledge they have a problem. Their mind will defend it and refuse to speak badly about it. They will say, "One day." But one day for most never comes. Seeing what it's like on the sober side of the fence can be rewarding.

We must learn to be vigilant minded. This means to be alert, watchful, and live with patience. The scripture verse on the back of this book, 1 Peter 5:8-9, says: "Be sober, be vigilant, because your adversary the devil walketh about as a roaring lion, seeking whom he may devour" To be sober and vigilant means to be well-balanced, self-disciplined, alert, and cautious. It's important to understand and look at the lives that alcohol has taken.

Next, I want to break down what alcohol does to the body. We can talk about its consequences, learn about them and make changes in our life. Work to stop the destruction before it destroys us. If you drink regularly, I recommend getting some blood work done. See how the body is functioning, and if you get some warning signs, it's time to change your lifestyle. Below are the problems that can be attributed to alcohol and its consumption.

Excessive and chronic alcohol consumption can contribute to a variety of health problems affecting different organs and systems in the body. Here is a comprehensive list of health issues associated with alcohol use:

1. **Liver Disorders:**
   - Fatty Liver Disease
   - Alcoholic Hepatitis
   - Cirrhosis
2. **Cardiovascular Issues:**
   - High Blood Pressure
   - Cardiomyopathy (weakening of the heart muscle)
   - Arrhythmias (irregular heartbeats)
   - Increased risk of stroke
3. **Cancer: Alcohol is linked to 7 fatal cancers**
   - Breast Cancer
   - Liver Cancer
   - Esophageal Cancer
   - Mouth, throat
   - Voice box
   - Colorectal Cancer
4. **Neurological Issues:**
   - Brain Atrophy
   - Cognitive Impairment

- Increased risk of dementia
- Wernicke-Korsakoff Syndrome (associated with thiamine deficiency)

5. **Mental Health Disorders:**
   - Depression
   - Anxiety
   - Increased risk of suicide
   - Alcohol Use Disorder (AUD)

6. **Gastrointestinal Problems:**
   - Pancreatitis
   - Gastritis (inflammation of the stomach lining)
   - Esophagitis (inflammation of the esophagus)

7. **Immune System Suppression:**
   - Increased susceptibility to infections

8. **Reproductive Issues:**
   - Impotence
   - Infertility

9. **Bone Health:**
   - Osteoporosis (reduced bone density)

10. **Metabolic Issues:**
    - Weight gain and obesity
    - Insulin resistance

11. **Respiratory Issues:**
    - Increased risk of pneumonia
    - Acute respiratory distress syndrome (ARDS)

12. **Sleep Disorders:**
    - Disruption of sleep patterns

13. **Increased Risk of Accidents:**
    - Unintentional injuries and accidents

14. **Alcohol Poisoning:**
    - Acute and potentially fatal condition due to high levels of alcohol in the bloodstream
15. **Social and Behavioral Consequences:**
    - Relationship problems
    - Employment issues
    - Legal problems

After the first month of everything I researched and learned I didn't want to be another statistic. The enjoyment of alcohol is way more destructive than rewarding, after you learn the facts and consequences.

I was a boozer for 34 years, and I got out. It's almost like being incarcerated for that long. Why do I say and believe this? Because that's how long it took me to hit my final rock bottom. I realized the trap was real and was out to destroy me.

It's a slow process. It's not immediate. For some It takes years and years to get to your rock bottom, and it's a lot harder to get out the longer you've been drinking. The potion was developed not to kill you right away, but it does take 24 years off your lifespan, when you drink regularly.

If you ever get the chance, see the movie *Flight* with Denzel Washington. It's a movie about an alcoholic who doesn't want to die as an alcoholic in society. He decides to put himself in jail, where he is safe from the deadly alcohol trap. In the end he purposely incarcerates himself to stop himself from his addiction and the madness. And for a lot of people, it's either get locked up to break the chains or fight your way out and get the help you need.

I finally got the help I needed and am forever in debt to the prayers and the mental health providers that got me out of the alcoholic shackles.

I want to dedicate this chapter to a friend of mine who was in the trap and is in prison for accidentally killing two people near a bar district in El Paso, Texas. It was a night of heavy drinking alcohol that completely robbed his life (Eduardo Sandoval). I pray for you often—that you are doing okay in prison and when you get out, I hope to see you and have a talk. Another one whose life was taken away due to the trap of alcohol. He didn't know alcohol was going to get him locked up and in jail for the rest of his life. Others are lucky, while some are not, and get devoured by alcohol's evil works.

Steal, kill, and destroy is the agenda that alcohol wants to accomplish. In my first year sober, I started realizing that not everyone drinks like I did. Some can control it and live a healthy life, and others keep falling deeper and deeper into alcoholic addiction. Stopping was hard work, with ups and downs. Here are three main areas to be aware of with long term use.

- Steal: Alcohol is out to steal friendships, close and far apart—from family members to old high school friends. It will work to get in between and take them away. Also, it will steal your money—from the days of waking up and checking your bank account or losing your wallet. It will do its best to steal from you. You can think of all the things it has stolen from you over the years while consuming.
- Kill: It will kill relationships to the point of no return. I have many of those. I stopped talking to people that were close to me, because of the

alcohol. It can be other things in your life it is working to kill—your health, your mind—alcohol is always working to kill what gets in its path.

- Destroy: It will destroy marriages. It will work to destroy your health. It will work to destroy your family. The steal, kill, and destroy list works hand in hand. It can steal, then destroy and eventually kill. I will make it clear—eventually, it will catch up to you. Being in your 30's, 40's and 50's and acting like you are 25, catches up to you like a thief in the night. But some just must go through it themselves. Some don't even wake up to see what their potential could have been. The steal, kill and destroy is different for everyone, but the reality is alcohol will affect your life in these areas every time.

The rest of this chapter, I will add all the guides you will need to get help—this is the go-to chapter for help immediately, with phone numbers as your guide. In chapter 9, I have a 30-day alcohol break to start right away as well. See what you think will work for you—take the step.

In the last 10 years of my drinking, we would count the lives lost to alcohol each year, and then, toward the end, we realized the numbers kept getting higher and closer to friends and family. Driving in the car one day, Jaymie told me, "I miss my friend," and with a moment of silence, I knew who it was— a good friend who lost the battle to alcohol, amongst other health issues. Turning 40, and then 50, I was hearing of people passing, and we all knew what the cause was, but it always kind of got pushed under the rug, and no one talked about it. It was in those times I was glad to be out, and knew I didn't want to end up like that.

There were times in my late 30s I knew I had a problem and would seek help, yet for whatever reason, I could never get the help I needed. See, it must come from you to stop. But if you see someone and they ask for help, please take every step to get that person help. I always kept quiet and didn't want to burden anyone, so I tried a few times to get help and reach out to a couple of people but never made the connection. That's the sad thing about any addiction: if we want help, it's as if everyone looks the other way. In the end we must want to help ourselves and do anything to get it.

Toward the last years of my addiction, I lost a lot of friendships along the way and remember them saying, "You need help." I was already consumed by the alcohol—it had already changed my mental state—and I didn't care or pay attention. From the early pages of Genesis to Revelation, it's noted that the good things God created will be attempted to be killed, stolen and destroyed by the enemy. Truly the work of the evil one—that is why many call alcohol the devil's potion.

I'm going to work to jump in now to get you the help you need so you can enjoy the good things life promises. Right here is the time to say: God created life with a purpose. If you don't believe in God, right now is probably the time to start. Indulging in alcohol will only take it all away.

There are a couple of things we can do. In this book, in chapter 9, I have developed a 30-day alcohol break. You can work to follow this and really commit to it each day. The second thing you can do is: get your phone or get in front of a computer. If you have bad shakes, wake up and drink, or need to drink to get an appetite, you can do a few things—seek an outpatient program or go inpatient—depending on what will work better for you. They both will help you get to where you need to be.

Some can quit cold turkey and never look back. If you have years in it you will more than likely need to get help. You may stop a few times, for 30 to 60 days, but if you really want to stop, you need help from an outside source.

If you are struggling, going back and forth, quitting and starting—it will be hard to get out. I would tell people about my last days on the sauce, and they wouldn't believe me. My brain literally would do what it wanted and take me to get what it wanted. It was like being possessed and just doing what the alcohol wanted—and that was to drink.

Here are important contacts you can reach out to that are 24/7 (the best gift you will ever give yourself is reaching out or making a call and taking back your life).

The first one I would like to add is www.recovery.org the first tab is Find a Rehab Center. The list includes all location in this network all over the country. Here is the phone #888-987-7852 as well.

If you or someone you know is struggling with alcohol abuse and needs immediate assistance or support, here are some more resources:

1. **National Helpline (SAMHSA):**
   - Phone: 1-800-662-HELP (1-800-662-4357)
   - Or Lifeline - Text 988 or you can call 988
   - Confidential, free, 24/7 helpline operated by the Substance Abuse and Mental Health Services Administration (SAMHSA).

- This confidential, free, 24/7 helpline has trained professionals and can provide information, support, and referrals for individuals and families facing substance abuse and mental health issues.

2. **Alcoholics Anonymous (AA):**
   - Phone: Varies by location. Search online for the specific number to your area.
   - Meeting Guide App: Download in the Google Play or Apple App Store (Look for the blue circle with a white chair logo.)
   - The app provides local meeting info and addresses.
   - AA is a fellowship where people share their experiences, strength, and hope to support each other in alcohol recovery.
   - Most cities have 24-hour local AA contact information through their website.

3. **National Institute on Alcohol Abuse and Alcoholism (NIAAA) Alcohol Treatment Navigator:**
   - Phone: 1-855-367-9464
   - The Alcohol Treatment Navigator, provided by NIAAA, offers information and resources to help individuals and families find evidence-based treatment options for alcohol use disorders.
   - Offers personalized guidance and support in finding treatment facilities and programs tailored to individual needs.

4. **Crisis Text Line:**
    - Text "HELLO" to 741741
    - You will receive a reply with a link to a website containing information to help with substance and alcohol abuse, suicide prevention and more.
    - Free, confidential, 24/7 support via text message for individuals in crisis, including those struggling with alcohol abuse. Trained crisis counselors offer confidential support and can help connect individuals to additional resources or services.
5. **Local Mental Health Hotlines:**
    - Many cities and countries operate 24-hour crisis lines for mental health and substance support. hotlines that offer support and referrals for individuals experiencing alcohol abuse or mental health crises.
    - Search Google for: "local mental health hotline [your city/country]".
    - 988 Is a crisis help line you can text or call.

These helplines are staffed by trained professionals who can provide support, information, and referrals to appropriate resources for individuals struggling with alcohol abuse. It's important to reach out for help if you or someone you know is facing alcohol-related challenges, as support and treatment options are available.

I mentioned AA (Alcoholics Anonymous), in your local city. There is also Narcotics Anonymous (NA), which will help if you are using more than just alcohol on a regular basis. If you go to the app store on your phone, you can download the NA app as well. There is also Al Anon for family members who struggle.

Here are some meetings that you can find online, or through text, phone, or web:

- AA Online Meetings General Page, this is usually the go to for online meetings.
  - http://aa-intergroup.org/
- AA Email Meetings
  - https://aa-intergroup.org/oiaa/meetings/?formats=Email
- AA Text Chat Meetings
  - https://aa-intergroup.org/oiaa/meetings/?formats=Chat
- AA Audio Video Meetings
  - https://aa-intergroup.org/oiaa/meetings/?formats=Video
- AA Website Discussion Meetings
  - https://aa-intergroup.org/oiaa/meetings/?formats=Forum
- AA Telephone Meetings
  - https://aa-intergroup.org/oiaa/meetings/?formats=Telephone
- LGBT AA Meetings
  - https://aa-intergroup.org/oiaa/meetings/?types=LGBTQIAA%2B

- Deaf and Hard of Hearing AA
  - https://aa-intergroup.org/oiaa/meetings/?
    types=Deaf%20%2F%20Hard%20of%
    20Hearing
- NA Web Meetings
  - https://www.na.org/meetingsearch/text-
    results.php
- NA Phone Meetings
  - https://www.na.org/meetingsearch/text-
    results.php
- Unity Recovery Individual and Family Meetings
  - https://unityrecovery.org/digital-recovery-
    meetings
- Al-Anon Meetings via phone
  - https://al-anon.org/al-anon-meetings/electronic-
    meetings/#Phone_Meetings (You can click on
    Skype, Facebook Messenger, Zoom, Bulletin
    Board, WhatsApp, Email.)
- In the Rooms
  - https://www.intherooms.com/home/category/
    community-and-meetings/

There really is something for anyone who truly wants help. See, I wish that when I was in my darkest hours, I had the help. I know there are many that want it and just don't know where to turn.

Even on Facebook, you can look up group pages like *Sober Sessions, Alcohol Is Not My Problem Anymore,* or *AA: The 12 steps*, and usually, a lot of other pages will come up for individuals looking for help. We have our Facebook page called *"The Hard Truth: Stopping Alcohol"*.

You must want to stop. If you're not ready or don't want help, it's not going to work for you. A lot of times, there must be a rock bottom for someone to get the help they need.

Next is a chapter to a better life—and what is expected if you are going to stop after years on the sauce.

4

TAKE THE FIRST STEPS TO A BETTER LIFE.

YOU WON'T REGRET IT!

Taking the first steps to a better life is really what it is all about. Who wouldn't want to go sober from alcohol and want a better life? Who wouldn't want to live away from substances that we turn to for some sort of mental relief? We as humans, have turned to cigarettes, vape pens, beer, wine, and pills, to help deal with day-to-day stress. We try to ignite the areas in our brain with these products and feel somehow it will help us. The hard truth is that by using long-term, you will see some repercussions from those vices. These items do not help us but are only hurting us.

As we get older, our bodies start to break down, and the real problems from them begin. We need to realize that it's all created to get us addicted and make millions for the distributors that create these products. The ups and downs, and the courage to stop is worth it long term.

Our minds are created to crave and want stimulation. Turning to substances for stimulation is what destroys us faster than normal living. Finding outlets for stimulation and our minds is key.

If we want change we need to understand that we have to change our thoughts. Have a new set of assumptions and beliefs. We must have a paradigm shift to a new thought process. Our mind is connected to our heart by 18 or so inches. And to have heart means to create courage and emotion. Have a newfound perspective an Aha moment. Repeat yourself to having changing thoughts and repeatedly changing our views. Helping the subconscious take over to change what we believe in, and it will create a new beginning and opportunity. Replace the old thought pattern with new thoughts and attitudes. Once all this happens you can start the change and process into a new type of life.

One Day I was standing in line at a convenience store while the person in front of me was buying 4 quarts of Busch beer, the first thought in my head was to think of Bill Wilson of Alcoholics Anonymous and how he would work to talk to drunks and help them. I was there at one time, buying my tall cans to go drink them. It's in those times, you realized that being sober is something to be proud of—and I was happy to have made it to a year and a half.

The thoughts and emotions at times of feeling confused and lost, and then I would get the moments of when it counts. Shedding some tears here and there, knowing that this is going to be the best of my remaining life—sober and free from any mind-altering substance.

I want to refer you to a Facebook page that I recommend. After reaching out to the creator of the page *Alcohol Is Not my Problem Anymore*. I asked Mr. Vig Adams' to use the *13 Steps to Sobriety*. It's a public group where you can ask and get answers immediately. Here are his 13 steps to sobriety that are helpful. You can find more details about these 13 steps on the front of his social media page in the tabs at the top. Also, under the "Files" near the top is an abundance of information you can download for guidance and help. He also has a book in one of the downloads, called the Vig Book.

By Vig Adams (Alcohol is Not My Problem Anymore)

Here are the 13 steps that I found most beneficial to facilitate my own recovery that I believe we must take to be best prepared to take on sobriety and succeed.

1. Seek Help!

Talk with your doctor and or a health professional about your desire and need to quit drinking alcohol. Detoxing from an addiction can be very risky and very serious medical emergencies can arise and a doctor can advise you best *before* you attempt to quit drinking. Even if you are simply thinking about the health ramifications of sobriety, you most definitely want to talk with a health professional.

2. Get rid of it! ALL of it!

All your alcohol and any other preferred substance(s) and any and all substances that could substitute for the addictive substance. Including over the counter and pet medications!

3. Do it for you!

DO NOT quit just because someone tells you to…you *MUST* own this new chapter in your life and create an unwavering commitment to quitting for good.

4. Have Support

A rock-solid team of people you trust to support your recovery is crucial. Partner, Family, Doctor, Trusted Friend,

Mentor, Sponsor, Clergy, Lawyer etc. as well as a program you can join and participate in meetings and discussions. Therapists and Psychiatrists can help us navigate the more difficult mental corridors of our addiction.

5. People, Places and Things.

Avoid past places, activities and old drinking buddies that are directly connected to your drinking past. It is absolutely essential that you remove yourself from anything and anyone that shares your past addiction.

6. Exercise every day.

Cardio, yoga, gym, go for a walk, bike, swim and stretching are wonderful ways to reconnect with our ability to move around, be active and have fun.

7. SLOW DOWN!!

Take it slow! Rushing through your day only invites anxiety. Do your tasks slowly and do them well. Slowing down invites calmness you so desperately need right now.

8. Just say NO!

Not just to your drug(s) of choice but to obligations and demands that could overtask you especially in the early days of recovery.

9. Learn to Substitute

Almost everything and anything that was associated with your addiction can be substituted with healthier choices.

10. Alone Time

This step is very important. Take time to chill out and relax. Learn to manage your thoughts and emotions while alone and by yourself.

11. Pamper Yourself.

Hot baths, lotions and oils, new clothes, haircut and good grooming. Try a new cologne or perfume.

12. Hobbies

Resume old hobbies and activities or even better try some new ones.

13. Go to Meetings

Group meetings, ZOOM meetings, AA, SMART, one-on-ones with a counselor, clergy, sponsors, mentors or trusted friends will be paramount in helping you navigate the turbulent early days of recovery and will also help in maintaining your sobriety in the long run.

When I go through all of these, I like to focus on #5: people, places and things. I truly think this is the #1 thing to help stay sober, especially in the beginning. You must get rid of all three. I see so many posts on Facebook in all the sober pages posting, "I am starting over after 90 days sober." They relapsed and broke because they didn't have a plan to stay sober. They didn't have a foundation. And for most of them, it all leads to being at the wrong place at the wrong time.

To completely stay sober, you need to drop the bad influences in your life. I had a friend early in my sobriety that wanted to come in town and stay for a funeral of our mutual friend. It was so early in my recovery that I said no—not that I didn't want him to come stay with me, but I was so fresh and green to this sober stuff, I didn't want anything to mess up my progress.

You want a better life? It must be by any means necessary not to go back into the alcohol trap. Also, if you have friends that come in town, let them know right away that you are sober and can go have lunch at a place that does not serve alcohol.

That is the best recommendation that I would give. Don't set yourself up for the mistake of being at the wrong place at the wrong time.

All of these steps are super helpful and will get you to help yourself on your journey. The best way to keep sober for me was getting a routine. I do work a lot, but it helps me stay busy and keeps me out of the trap.

Meetings can be important, and while I didn't do a lot of meetings my first year, I did meetings online, and they were helpful on days I just felt low in my sobriety. It helped me get back up, knowing that I am not alone on this journey and that many are seeking life without alcohol—and are successful.

You will hear people with 3 years sober, then some with one week sober. It's good to hear that you are not alone in this, and others are and have gone through what you are experiencing. It only gets better…

"Anyone in recovery knows that isolation is the biggest enemy."

— *IVAN MOODY*

You have to want it so bad that you will do what it takes. Living a life feeling like crap every other day is not a way to live. Everyone should do what works for them—find it and just do it. You won't regret it, and it will be the best years you have in your life. You need to struggle now to get clean and enjoy the rest of your life.

As addicts to alcohol, we think, "Enjoy now—we only live

once," when we will struggle later in life if we just live to enjoy now. Struggle with health issues that we were not supposed to live with. They say hindsight's a bitch—well, you don't have to deal with hindsight if you fight now for whatever it takes to live your best life.

We must not let the alcohol kill us. That will be a blessing, because for the rest of your life, you can grow. Grow to the person you were always meant to be.

5

THE AFTERMATH

WHILE ENJOYING THE REBIRTH OF LIFE

I don't ever want to drink again, knowing that I fell for the trap and got sucked in. It's not something to play around with. Alcohol is one of the worst substances on the planet and is not made for human consumption. It is also the only substance that can enter the cells core and start destroying it from within. Other drugs attach to the surface of cells—alcohol passes into the cell.

In the body, alcohol turns into acetaldehyde, which can damage your DNA and prevent your body from repairing the harm it's caused. This is why alcohol is linked to seven fatal types of cancer. The toxic buildup of acetaldehyde can turn into acetate, which is a straight poison.

When you learn and understand the destruction alcohol causes, at a cellular level. You can begin to realize where you are headed with continuous drinking. Once you stop beating yourself up with alcohol and get the shackles taken off, here is what to expect.

My first 30 days were great. Sober friends would say, "It

only gets better." Some would say, "Go to meetings; they will help you." While I did attend some online meetings and a few in person, I found that old passions became new passions. So, you too can rediscover an old passion and get back into it.

For me, it was skateboarding. Finding groups of people in their fifties who still skateboarded was a relief. While some think it's just for kids, it's one of the best workouts you will ever experience—you use all your muscles, and improve balance, coordination, and agility. See, it does get better. Just imagine taking off a cast and being able to breathe again—getting fresh air to your brain that you have been missing. That's how I can describe it.

But at the same time, I was trying to find a sleep pattern—only sleeping 4 to 5 hours at a time. Medication may be necessary in the first six months to a year. I needed help finding a sleep pattern. I found out that creating a nighttime routine helped me get to bed: eating a little something, drinking tea, or sometimes taking a shower. Go through the steps and figure out what works for you. For me, it was sleepy tea and some cereal. I also took magnesium glycinate or magnesium oxide supplements to help me sleep.

I would also get headaches—yes, your brain gets wacked out by ethanol. Expect headaches for the first six months to a year—not every day, but some days more than others. The headaches were usually in the back of my head. I believe the brain stem was working to repair itself from all the damage.

Dealing with emotions and feelings—learning to deal with them instead of turning to booze—was a whole process. In the first six months, you start to think of all the friendships you lost and the problems that came from drinking. That's when the 12 Steps can help with this. **Step** 9 says:

"**Make** direct **amends** to such people wherever possible, except when to do so would injure them or others." This can help us start the healing process from the poison.

I didn't really work this step as much as I should have, but I think I did it in my own ways. Being clean led me to the people I needed to make amends with. The relationships I needed to rebuild were with my sons, Caleb and Brayden, and my mom. Believe it or not, even the relationship I was already in was like starting over and being in a new relationship. Jaymie and I could talk, and we became close in sobriety. Having a sober partner and living a sober life with them was an important factor in staying clean. If you can't keep trying to help the person that needs it, there are also Al-Anon meetings for people living with someone suffering with addiction.

I had almost lost those relationships with the people closest to me. And believe it or not, they came together in the way they needed to—after I stopped drinking.

I was really able to do it on my own by staying busy—working and getting my mind back by dropping alcohol. I created that paradigm shift that Really changed how I perceived alcohol. The companies pump ads out to inter our subconscious mind and make us believe that it's all ok. My mind had started to change, and I was processing my thoughts differently. With that said, the things you get done when you don't drink are amazing. I would get more things done in one week than I would in months. At the end of the day, sometimes I would think, "How the hell would I get stuff done and drink in the day and still try to work?"

In the aftermath of the first year, things would come to me about all the years of drinking. I would ask myself how did I avoid getting myself in big trouble with the law or even driving and hurting someone? The other thing that was circling was just years and years of going out and a lot of those memories coming back and reliving them. I asked myself, WTF? How are you still alive?

During my recovery I drank a lot of green tea and also took liver supplements—those probably have helped me. But when talking to doctors, they said it's all genetics. It's different for everyone. The impact is not the same for each person. It affects everyone differently.

Toward the end of my drinking days, I was having too many blackouts—forgetting things and not really caring about myself or anyone else. I ended up in the hospital and had my stomach drained for two days due to an abscess that the alcohol had caused in my insides. I later found out that the brother of my counselor at the outpatient center I went to had passed away from something similar to what I had. I was spared by the grace of God—I really started counting my blessings.

When in the trap, alcohol will make you believe that it's okay. You'll say, I've got this under control, when it's still taking you on its ride to get faster to your grave, completely taking over your thoughts and belief system. It wasn't until around the 10th month that I started to realize this.

In the aftermath, you start losing and gaining weight. I was up and down during the first 10 months, turning to oatmeal cookies and sweets. Then I got the dreaded sciatica issue that pushed me to a healthier diet. I wanted to build myself up—not tear myself down with sugar and junk food.

Your biggest success story in life when going sober will be that you have a clear mind and feel like a completely grounded human again. The thoughts of how you would drink still linger and it may cross your mind to have one, but you know that it will only bring you to that dark place that you were once in—and you are way past that point in your life to go back.

One of the things that I noticed in my first year is: some people can have a few drinks with dinner, some can go out with friends, have a few beers, and call it a night. That's what really makes us all different when consuming.

For the alcoholic, we chase the high that the alcohol gives us, and we can't stop until we are at the point of passing out or blacking out. That's the big difference. If you can recognize that you are not one of those people who can have a drink and do not think about it for a year or even months, then you are not an alcoholic. But if you turn to it for everything you do, or just to feel normal, then you need to realize you have a problem and need to stop. I'll be the first to tell you that you have a problem and don't see it.

At the year-and-a-half mark after I stopped drinking, I started to realize I was thinking better, and my thoughts had become more rational. There were moments when I would be sitting on my couch, and the lights and colors seemed clearer. The images around me became vibrant. It was almost like the haze and residue of alcohol in my mind were finally dissolving, and my brain was starting to return to the normal state it was supposed to be in.

There is a saying: Going sober for some can be easy, it's living that's hard. We used to turn to alcohol for our worries, but it never really helped. I started realizing that the years that had passed almost seemed like a different life. From relation-ships to my sons' being born, they all seemed like a past life.

You can also start and leave those memories in the memory file and learn to start new chapters and new memories with a sober mind. We all go through things in life that are part of each other's walks and can say we all help each other to the next chapters and seasons of our lives. Even if it was temporary, it was those seasons that shaped our futures.

It wasn't until the end of my first year of sobriety that I really began to see what alcohol had done to me. I could process thoughts better. I still had some brain fog and was dealing with the repercussions, but I was gaining better thoughts and more positive ones. No hangovers—and knowing that I was adding years to my life was a good feeling. I don't know what the long-term effects will be, but I do know that the one-year mark was a game-changer.

Jaymie was taking off in her sobriety, hitting two years and earning certifications with Davita and getting promoted—and we discussed that it couldn't have happened if we had kept drinking. I was working to get my life coach certifications and writing this book. It proved that once you take ethanol out of the equation, things start adding up for the better. It's not overnight, but it's a gradual sense of awakening and peace that comes with knowing life is only getting better.

6

THE EMOTIONAL ROLLER COASTER

You have reprogrammed your mind with alcohol, and there comes a time when we need to leave childish things behind and grow up. The bible says it best in 1 Corinthians 13:11: "When I was a child, I spoke like a child, I thought like a child, I reasoned like a child. When I became a man, I put away childish things". And in the same way for females, you stop to become the women God created you to be.

Over many years of drinking your mind is reprogrammed: it's the booze that makes me feel this way and think this way. We have associated alcohol with so many of our day-to-day routines that it's adapted and embedded in your mind. So, how do I change this thought pattern? What needs to take place? Understand that it's all gone sour in your mind, yet you can't see it—it feels normal to drink for every occasion. Once it's gone sour, it won't ever be the same. It's like the minute hand of a clock—once it moves forward, you can't take it back. It's done.

Just know whether it's one day or ten days, you can't go

back. So, it's best to go through the struggles and work to understand them.

Take some time to ask yourself:

- Why do I always turn to drink?
- Why do I do this at this time each day or every other day?
- Why am I thinking about drinking? Or, come Thursday it's beer 30.
- What is the reason I drink? Can I stop for a year and not think or need it?

Once you have those conversations with yourself, you will realize your mind was programmed this way from the years of drinking. The perfect example is the holidays—the sights and sounds are such a trigger that it becomes a mental struggle. Thoughts like, back then I would go there, or I'd do this on this day, or this is the perfect time to drink.

You must realize that it's alcohol that has programmed your mind. It's grooved and embedded. You must create new thoughts and embed new memories. Go get some good food, take a brisk run, or hit the gym. Find what works for you.

I would go to the skatepark and skate my ass off—not the biggest tricks, but just enough to get the heart pumping and understand that you do whatever it takes, but just do it. That snake is in the parking lot doing push-ups, waiting to come at you any chance it gets. The more you resist alcohol, the more it will flee.

James 4:7: "Submit yourselves therefore to God. Resist the devil, and he will flee from you."

This is powerful—and it works every time. Easier said than done, right? But the more times you resist, the easier it gets. You will find a way to get past it. Do whatever it takes. They don't say "fight the good fight" for nothing.

Breaking normal thought patterns is key. Change up your room. Redecorate your house. Sell the things that remind you of the boozer days. Take a new route home—as many times as you need. If you must move, move and start fresh. Do things differently: shower in a different pattern. Sounds ridiculous, but you need to reprogram your mind. Make your bed a different way. It's these little things you do that will make the difference in the end.

The back cover of this book has the best scripture, and we should hold fast to it daily: 1 Peter 5:8 "Be sober-minded, be watchful, be vigilant; because your adversary the devil walks about like a roaring lion, seeking whom he may devour."

The more sober minded we are, the more we can live the life we are meant to live. They don't say "take it one day at a time" for nothing. This too shall pass. If it's a hard day, this too shall pass.

One of the biggest things I had to overcome were the emotions I was dealing with. Just dealing with people—sometimes it seemed like they were trying to make things difficult for me. But why?

I had to come to a common ground and understand I can't change them—I can only change myself. And by changing myself, I can get past what I am experiencing with the lives around me. So, if they can't change—not a big deal, I can change how I perceive them.

Sound selfish? Well, sometimes you must be to avoid falling into the lair of the booze trap ever again.

You need to find what works for you and stick to it. Some people will mess up a million times before they get it right. Just don't let that lead to a life where you are forced to live your last days in and out of hospitals, wondering how much time you have left. Break the chains and make this your best life.

In the later days of the second year of my sobriety, I had many thoughts of wanting to help others—but I didn't know how. I'm thankful that I wrote this book, because it will eventually help someone who needs it.

"The Hard Truth"—that's what came to me as I thought about it. I planned to name it: "The Hard Truth: How to Get Alcohol-Free on an Intoxicated Earth." Then I decided on just The Hard Truth! "Stopping Alcohol".

There is no easy or right way to break from alcohol. You must dig deep and meet it head-on. It was easy to drink the problems away—but to face them head-on? That's the true sober warrior mentality. Facing life sober does get easier.

Knowing that I added years to my life was a positive thought. If I kept drinking, it would take up to 24 years of my life away. I was thankful. Getting closer to two years without drinking, I was thankful for how my emotions had changed and how I had become a more understanding person.

You can also begin to feel what life is supposed to feel like not drowning your true feelings and emotions. A lot of us had family members who drank or used drugs, but we need to break that generational curse if we want a better life.

It had been a rollercoaster of thoughts to this point, but I finally found the meaning in "one day at a time" and "let go and let God". For today, I understand I don't have control over others, only myself. Sometimes, I need to let go. God will work it out the way it needs to happen. It will be dealt with, on His terms.

In my sober time, 1 year and 7 months, I still had days where I struggled with emotions and feelings. But it was in those frustrations that I reminded myself: Okay, I have no control over the situation. I can either feel upset about it, or I can let God help me deal with it. I knew if I let it go and let God, it would work itself out. Stepping back and learning to deal with it the next day helped me resolve issues a lot better. In the past, when I was frustrated and angered, I would turn to alcohol to suppress my feelings. I came to realize it was not taking them away but delaying the actual problem from being resolved. We need to understand that we don't need alcohol to get through life's realities. Or drink to relax because we had a long day and deserve it.

Take some deep breaths and be okay with it. It's going to pass. It just needs time to unfold the way it needs to unfold. These techniques worked for me.

Another realization that helped me as I approached two years alcohol-free was being able to process my thoughts a lot better. I was dealing with my emotions differently. The emotional roller coaster was still lingering. But one thing I can count on, is NOT being hungover or feeling like crap from trying to drink my emotions away.

The light of life was finally shining through. It felt great knowing that if I wasn't drinking, life was making sense. God as I knew him was more present, and I was able to find what the creator of all of this is all about. Another tool I used when I was feeling worried or frustrated is to count backwards 5,4,3,2,1 to remind myself to stop, re-gather my thoughts, analyze the situation, and process it. As regular drinkers we tend to act irrationally and impulsively. We drink and the frontal lobe of the brain shuts off. Counting backwards will help us put things into perspective and gather our thoughts. I recommend giving this a try with really anything in life that can be upsetting or frustrating. It helps process the mental state and calms you down.

In recovery, we also must consider something called Post-Acute Withdrawal Syndrome—PAWS. This can last months or even years. It's all caused by consistent use and abuse of alcohol and drugs. The typical time frame is 6 months to 2 years, but I have heard of it coming and going even longer. It usually peaks around 3 months after you stop drinking or using drugs. The effects will diminish over time if you stay away from the use of any addictive substances. The main symptoms are:

- Anxiety
- Inability to handle stress
- Inability to solve problems
- Inability to think clearly
- Inability to concentrate
- Repetitive thinking
- Memory problems
- Emotional over reaction or numbness
- Depression
- Sleep disturbances

To recover from problems caused by our addictions and PAWS we need to completely abstain from drugs or alcohol.

Here are Ways to work and stabilize "Paws symptoms":

- Talking to someone helps recognize our thoughts.
- Identify your feelings. Why are you feeling this way?
- What can we do right now to improve our situation?
- Nutrition- eating right and making sure we are getting the nutrients we need. Nutrients help our mind and thoughts. Take good multivitamins.
- Relaxation and meditation
- Journaling
- Learn to feel good about yourself

The Hard Truth is—you need to create new mental pathways to figure out what works for you. Possibly medications that are non-addictive to dealing with life's misfortunes. Meet with a mental health provider who can guide and help you curb some of these symptoms. There are also natural remedies and vitamins that can help. Some herbal remedies I tried was Rhodiola. People use rhodiola for fatigue, anxiety, depression, stress, and many other conditions, but there is no good scientific evidence to support any of these uses. When stopping there is a healing period, and we need to learn that growth happens with time. Creating a balanced lifestyle with a support network can help us achieve a better life. Working to slow physical and mental stress allows psychological growth.

7

THE HARD TRUTH

What does it take to get sober? People around you are not going to see what you see or know what you are going through. This is your journey, and you must understand that it's your responsibility to focus on it. If someone else wants to drink and kill themselves slowly, then that is their journey and their decision.

I had to come to terms with the fact that alcohol is a billion-dollar industry, and they are going to get into your subconscious mind and make you believe that it is good or ok to be a part of. The packaging, the advertising, celebrity endorsements, billboards... It's all fuel to keep this billion-dollar industry alive. Behind all that is a Class A addictive substance that will change your mind and your reward system down to the core of your body chemistry. Dopamine areas of the brain become damaged to the point that the only thing that makes sense is alcohol. It affects the fight-or-flight areas of the brain, making you think you need it to survive, like water or food. Your brain will convince you that you need it. But when you turn to it, you are only killing your insides and getting closer to your grave—years before your time. It is never discussed and seems to be the hidden agenda of these companies. They never discuss the reality of what the substance does to so many, it kills 3 million people every year worldwide. The companies used the perfect chemistry to keep you coming back week after week and take your money to add to their billions each year.

I mean, if that's what you want to go through in life, then I suggest you keep drinking: kidney problems, liver problems, in and out of dialysis centers, seeing doctors on a regular basis to see what they can do to save your life. Sitting in a dialysis chair three times a week for four hours isn't how I want to spend the rest of my life and my time. You must think long term—see where your life is heading and how you want to spend the rest of your days. We are not promised forever.

This chapter is called The Hard Truth for a reason. Alcohol will lead you to three things: hospitals, jail, or an early grave—not to mention all the personal problems and stress it will cause you along the way. You must want to commit to helping yourself 110%, not 100%. That extra 10% is to make sure you stop. You will also have to want to stop. No one will do it for you. You must get to the point where you feel like you are underwater, desperate to get to the surface and take a breath of air. That's what it feels like if you're addicted and are trying to decide if you need help. When the threshold of pain is greater than the reward of the substance, it's time to stop. You become sick and tired of being sick and tired.

If you know you are, then do whatever it takes. Get into an outpatient or inpatient program. Get some medication to help you stop. Talk to a healthcare provider and see what they can do to take away the cravings. The Hard Truth is that people are not going to believe in the things that you do. You will see people suffer and hurt the ones around them through their drinking, and you can't control anyone but yourself.

That was the main message behind The Hard Truth—but the other is: I realized I drank for all those years, and the damage was done. My mind doesn't work like it would have if I had not drunk and there was no damage. Alcohol shrinks the white and gray matter in the brain, which connects different areas and allows them to communicate and exchange information. Alcohol will trick you into believing that nothing is happening and that you are fine. It isn't okay, and if you continue, it only gets worse. There comes a time that you will need to stop. If not, you will reap the consequences you create.

I also realized that by stopping, I was going to find the real person I was meant to be, and I could finally find myself. What's been hard is that even after a year or years alcohol-free, the thoughts I was having may linger and will mess with me to have a drink. Not that I ever want to drink, but it plays in the mind: "It's okay, everyone does it. It's safe as long as it's in moderation." That's what the advertisements want you to believe. But no—it doesn't work that way. Once you cross that line, the addiction will set in again and destroy or kill you. I have seen it happen. It has happened to friends I know personally.

If I eat healthily and work to stay healthy, I will enjoy the days I have left. I will still see people suffering around me, and all I can do is reach out and try to help. Most will not want help, until it's their time.

The Hard Truth is: What kind of life do you want? Is this how you want to keep living? The party must stop. The nonsense needs to stop. You feel good for a little while, then feel like crap later. That wasn't how I wanted to live my days —working or retired, I didn't want to live and be drinking all the time, feeling pain on my right side where my liver is. Different pains everywhere, wondering what they are.

There must come a time when you ask yourself, "Is this how I want to go out? Or do I want to keep living? A good friend, Malcolm Hunt, said:

"Once the fun isn't any fun, that's when things have to stop or change."

It's not fun anymore. Do you really want to be that old man trying to look like he's 30-years-old that can't seem to grow up? Or that person in their mid-life crisis? At any age, it's time to stop drinking. When is enough, when those thoughts cross your mind—"I need to make a change"—listen to them. People are not going to say, "Hey, I think you should stop or slow down." So, I am telling you: if you drink every day, every other day, or even drink all weekend, then yes, it's time to try a change and stop.

The Peter Pan syndrome needs to leave the building, and you should consider leading a new life. It won't be easy, but it will be well worth it. Your life isn't going to change by repeating the same stupid stuff. You are your thoughts, and you become your thoughts. So those thoughts need to change. Go to an AA meeting. Talk to a few who have stopped. Read some books like this one. There's a lot out there for men and women trying to stop drinking. Facebook groups that are full of non-drinkers. The people's testimonies are helpful—and soon, you can have your own. It all boils down to this: Do you want to change, or don't you?

Once you decide to change, make the steps. Talk to yourself and say, "Okay, what do I need to do?" Write what comes to your head and follow through with it.

Here are my Hard Truth Steps – A spin-off of the AA Twelve Steps:

1. Admitting that my life became ridiculous, and I have been an idiot. When I drink, I can't see how I am acting but people around me can. We need to realize that being hungover is your body trying to tell you how unintelligent you have been. Time to realize you're in the alcohol trap!

2. Know that when I drink, I look like an idiot and sound like an idiot. Drinking is not cool anymore. I can change everything about my drinking today. Work towards a Paridym Shift, a new thought belief system.

3. Make a hard decision to get yourself out of this nonsense.

4. Admit and write down how much of a moron I have been—all the stupid crap I have gotten myself into. Put it on paper so you can see black and white how much alcohol has ruined you. Do you like what you see in the mirror?

5. Tell someone you are close to how stupid you have been and ask them to help you stop being a loser. Or simply help yourself, no one can do it for you! The only one loosing is you, no one else suffers the consequences.

6. Try to become smarter when making choices and stop destroying yourself. As you age, alcohol is only going to create more problems for you! REGARDLESS!

7. Straighten my life out and work to be normal every day from this day forward.

8. Make a list of the people I have disrespected. Call or text them to say, "I am a result of bad choices." Tell them, "I don't want to bother you, but sorry for being so ignorant." Most importantly be true to yourself!

9. If you can't call them, you will need to accept the fact you lost them in your life, and they weren't meant to be in it anyway. Drop that thought at the curb and don't look back. If it's family, you can try, but if they don't want to talk, let it go. Try again later if you think they need more time.

10. Know that when I start acting like a moron, I need to tell myself to chill the F out. You're working to be on a different level and on a new path in life.

11. Know that it's not going to happen overnight, and life's better when I'm not drinking. I need to stick to it to see results no matter how hard it gets.

12. Reach out to people that can help me first and get the help I need to change my life. In helping myself I can work to help others—so you can pass the torch of helping someone become their true self.

These are my Hard Truth 12 steps. Sometimes it's best to be brutally honest with yourself and talk a little Hard Truth about what you have been up to. I challenge you to write down your 12 steps and how they relate to you. Make your own twist to the 12 steps and how they can best relate to you.

What worked for me was when I knew I had jacked up my life and was at rock bottom, I decided to call several places and asked if they had any outpatient opportunities and if I could set up an appointment. It wasn't until I went to two or three places that I found one that helped me. It was an outpatient opportunity that was every day, all day. I went home at night and went back at the same time every day. There were meetings. There were one-on-ones. You're around a lot of people stopping and doing the same thing as you are. The outpatient that helped me in El Paso, Texas, was Rio Vista Behavioral Health. It was a game changer for me. And in any city, there are places that will help you get your life on track. The world is too busy moving forward to wait on you or justify your rationing. You must want to hit the grind and get to it. Admit you are powerless over the addiction. Shape up or ship out. LET'S GO! DO PEP TALKS TO YOUSELF AND GET WITH IT! YOUR LIFE DEPENDS ON IT. Do you have any self-respect? Stop playing games with yourself and get the help you need. I may not be in front of you, but I am writing it on paper. Change is the best decision you will make for yourself and the people around you. The time has come, and it's in your hands to work to make that change.

Once, I walked down the aisle in the grocery store with my middle finger in the air. Why? Because I hate it. Learn to hate what it has done to you and the people around you. I watched movies related to alcohol or drug addiction and realized it's a pandemic and a sickness. Learn what's really going on. The movie that came out on Hulu, *Dope Sick*, talks about the opioid epidemic that has happened with OxyContin—the big pharma that was trying to make billions on addiction. In my mind I feel the alcohol companies are doing the same thing. They know how addictive ethanol can be, and they don't have any labels or any information to let people know the dangers. It causes seven fatal cancers, and all the horrible health effects of long-term use I have mentioned in this book. The Lancet (a prestigious weekly medical journal) published an article stating that no amount of alcohol is good for you, not even a glass of wine, which was previously thought to be good for your heart. This was considered the "French Paradox" and was later found not to be true according to The Lancet.

Risks Outweigh Benefits:

While moderate drinking was previously thought to have some health benefits, the study found that the potential risks of alcohol, particularly cancer, outweigh any potential benefits.

The Lancet weekly medical journal is published to make science widely available, to improve health and advance human progress. It publishes peer-reviewed research on clinical, public health, and global health topics.

No amount of alcohol is good for you. The World Health Organization recommends a label about the dangers of alcohol. Ireland, in 2026, will be the first country to legally mandate alcohol producers to provide a comprehensive warning on alcohol products. They will say in red: "There is a direct link between alcohol and fatal cancers" and "Drinking alcohol causes liver disease." This will be a first, and I hope all countries will follow. More advertisements should have more information about the dangers of it, and more people need to start talking about what the real problem is. I can't wait for the day when advertisements follow alcohol companies' ads telling the truth about alcohol's damaging effects.

Another good book I recommend is *Alcohol Explained* by William Porter. This book really goes into the details of what alcohol does—from the personal level to the complete life of the alcoholic. It really breaks down how bad it really is.

In quitting, you have to want it more than life itself. That's the truth. And if you do, you will need to find what works for you. For me, I couldn't stop unless I had medication to derail me from the addiction. And you can only find that with an inpatient or outpatient setting, or a provider that does counseling on addiction. This can be expensive but will help you get back on track and into the right life that you were meant to have. You can't keep doing the same things and expect different results. Try some AA meetings. There is also SMART Recovery. While in some cities you can only find meetings online. It is for everyone also including meetings to help first responders and families deal with addiction. This is an evidence-based recovery method grounded in cognitive behavioral therapy, that supports people with substance dependence or problem behaviors. Build and maintain motivation. Cope with urges and cravings. Manage thoughts, feelings, and behaviors.

You are also going to have to realize that alcohol—if you have drunk for many years—has pretty much reprogrammed your mind. Also, you could have the effects of genetic predisposition, which means it's already programmed in your mind and will be that much harder to stop. Alcohol creates pathways in the brain that will literally have to be reprogrammed and dealt with. It will take working to create new pathways, create new memories, and learn to deal with life head-on. Before, we would numb ourselves up with alcohol and it only makes the problem worse by never really confronting it or ignoring what we had caused. Fights or arguments with friends—or just plain making yourself look like an idiot more than likely occurs in a drunken state of mind. Alcohol changes the frontal lobe of the brain when consumed and alters the decisions that we make. If consumed heavily, it will be damaged and take a few years to get back on track. We have all heard of the drunk driver that was going down the freeway and killed someone. Their frontal lobe—the decision-making part of the brain—was turned off and they did not make a clear decision. I mentioned this a few times in this book, but I have to think the alcohol companies know what they are doing but look the other way knowing they are destroying people's lives.

Also, along your journey, when you get to a good sober point, you will be someone to help someone in need. That's like passing on the torch of a good deed. In AA, you can work to be a sponsor to someone and help them get past the addiction. Or, you can work to show how well you are doing—and when someone sees this, they will want that also for themselves. The Hard Truth—that's what it is. You can't get to the other side of the fence unless you face the hard truth and fight to get there. Do whatever it takes and don't give up. If you fall, get back up and keep going. There are a lot of people wanting to help—you just have to work to talk to them. Remember, you got this, and it will only work as much as you want to work it.

In closing, remember this: addiction in any form tears apart connections—the connection to who you really are. Addiction will also tear apart great friendships, tear apart marriages, and tear apart a family. It can even tear apart a whole community (for example, an opioid crisis). Addiction has us coming back a lot of times because of pain. It's a pain that we don't want to feel anymore. It can also be a pain that the addiction has started or caused. The pain you feel is in all of us, and some more than others. There is emotional pain, life's challenges of pain, worry, and confusion, with mental strain that feels like pain. And we just don't want to feel it anymore. So, we turn to the source that we feel solves the problem. But the further we fall into an addiction, the alcohol tells us we are better off just feeling nothing at all. So, we go numb, and our souls go numb. That's when the problem has set in, and it feels like there's no turning back. But the truth is—you can turn back. What path do you really want? Because you only have two. Face the pain head-on and find out who you really are or destroy yourself and end up in a box.

You need to realize pain is just pain—not good, not bad— just part of being a human being and being alive on this earth. A lot of times, going sober, the greatest things in your life can come out of it. If you're brave enough and willing to dig deep, you can work your way through it and overcome it. That's when the real miracle of your life begins, and we work to find the better version of ourselves that was lost for so long. It's never easy, but you must dig deep and want the problems to go away. It doesn't happen overnight—but once you get your head right, it's all worth the fight.

8

THE SPIRITUAL FACTS

I wanted to add my spiritual journey to help anyone who is looking to stop drinking alcohol and isn't sure what kind of spiritual help they may need. I was raised attending a Catholic church in El Paso, Texas. Every Sunday we got ready and went to church. I did my first communion and went to the required classes to have my first communion, at around 8 or 9 years old at St. Patrick's Cathedral in downtown El Paso. I credit the Catholic church for my spiritual foundation and have a lot of respect for Catholicism. I prayed a lot in church, and I went to confessions when I felt the need. I am a believer. Deep in my heart, I know and feel there is a God who created all of this.

Whether you want it or not, we all need some sort of spiritual help. Some people don't believe in a higher power, and some are flat-out atheists. I pray they realize that someone or something created all of this. How is it that you can think? How is it that you can make decisions, rationalize, and work to be alive? How perfect is the functioning of the human mind? The way your body is designed to live and walk the earth, the details of sight, the anatomy of your body and brain, and the food sources that have been created for human consumption are all a lot more than humans can begin to comprehend. Our little minds are nothing compared to the power of the Creator of this planet. If you look at the intricate detail of oxygen, the chemistry of life, and how every living being is connected in some way—you cannot deny there is a creator to all this immaculate precision of art and life on earth. On my journey, I had a few near-death experiences, and found that if you didn't believe in a higher power before, you will at that point. It's in our nature to want to live and be alive. But when your heart is beating at 150 beats a minute, you're in a hospital bed and everything is looking fuzzy, not wanting to leave this earth just yet—you more than likely will pray at some point.

When I was 20 years old, drinking and partaking in different illegal substances like marijuana—back then it wasn't legal in any state, like it is in some states today—and while drinking and not being in my right mind, I came across methamphetamine. Being irresponsible and immature, I tried it. One of the worst decisions I had made in my life. I'm not proud of it, and it's the first worst substance on the planet, alongside alcohol in my mind. It didn't agree with me, and it almost killed me. It's in those times you realize that there must be a higher power that heard my prayers and saved me. I fought to stay alive in a hospital bed for over 12 hours. I am lucky to still be here. I want to believe I have a purpose, and if it's to save one person, I did my job on this planet. I hope I can reach as many people as possible with this book—people who need help like I did. I had started drinking at a young age, going to Juarez, and it led up to that moment of staring death in the face and realizing life is short. I have seen too many in my 51 years, as I write this book, who didn't make it. I pray that they are in a better place and are helping do God's work—being free from the addiction that took their life.

It was at that time, being 20 years old, that I would spend the next year sober, thankful to be alive, and trying to find who God was. It was in prayer and seeing my life almost leaving me that I wanted to understand who this designer of life is. In that time, I felt a new existence. I wanted to learn who He or It was and how to find Him. It was during this time I went and asked to talk to the head priest at the Catholic church, and we talked about my journey of mistakes and almost dying. I talked about my curiosity in finding out who God really is and what it is all about. It was the next words that came out of his mouth that gave me the most respect for the Catholic church. He said, "Where you find God is where you need to be." It can be in the Catholic church or any church, but where you feel and find Him and want to be there—that's where you need to be.

After this meeting, I started looking into all religions—like Buddhism, the book of Mormon, Jehovah's witness, Pentecostal—I wanted to know who this God was and where I could find Him. I learned a lot at that time, and it was shortly after all of this that a friend of mine, who I met in high school, invited me to his church. Miguel Varela, who now has a prospering company in California, said, "Hey, come check out my church. It's got a live band and it's like literally going to a live show like *The Tonight Show*." I said, "Okay, when do we go?" He replied, "This Sunday, I'll pick you up." That Sunday I was ready, just as he said, and I was on my way to Abundant Living Church on the east side of El Paso.

This was in 1994 or 1995, and it wasn't the church it is today. It was the smaller building that is next to the

Abundant Church that exists today. Now there are three churches and expansions to other cities. It was during that time when I went that I felt something like no other. It was alive, it had something I needed, and it felt different. It was in one of the services when they did an alter call to accept Jesus—and I was in the front row. I wanted to know who this God is, and I will say it was something that came over me that day that only those who experience it understand. The best way to describe it is I felt warm and fuzzy, and something was inside of me. Whatever it was, I found where I needed to be.

The awesome part is, through all the following years, I would go, then stop going for a while—but every time I would go back, the warm feelings were there. It never leaves your side. Those who have experienced the feeling will understand and know.

My point is this: you can go on that journey and investigate the different religions or churches that are out there until you find your God. Where you find God is where you need to be. The thing that I found out in all the studies of religion or faith-based beliefs of a higher power is that it's all the same God. We can't see Him, we can't touch Him, but we can talk to Him—He is there with us. And we must understand that whatever your beliefs are, find a good church—like I found at Abundant Living Church—and stick to it. Your life will depend on it.

Abundant is a Christian church considered a non-denominational church that believes in Jesus Christ, who was born of the Virgin Mary and is the Son of God. You can find Him in a book, and that book is the Bible—a book that has been here for 3,400 years and will outlive all of us. In this book, you will find stories of everything you can imagine—motivation, strength, defeat, hope, perseverance, new beginnings, and endings.

Speaking of beginnings and endings, I recommend a book from the head pastor of Abundant Living Church, Charles Nieman, called *Endings & Beginnings*. The book is, as stated in the intro page, a story of how the Lord walked him through the trauma of the single greatest loss of his life: the death of his wife Rochelle. This book talks and walks you through endings and beginnings for anyone that has been through a heavy trauma. I found some things in my recovery from alcohol in the book that have helped me as well. I highly recommend it, and you can find it at charlesnieman.com.

The most inspiring part for me in the book is as follows: what feels like the end is often the beginning. When you stop alcohol, you can at times feel lost—like it's the end of something that was there for you. And the end of alcohol is only the beginning of a better life that you had lost and now can find again. The truth is that alcohol was never your friend—it was your enemy. Don't let the enemy have a seat at your table. In the Bible, John 10:10 says, "The thief comes only to steal, kill and destroy; I came so that they might have life and have it more abundantly." You see, the verses in this 3,400-year-old book will live forever. They were written through the mind of the Creator, into the minds of men of this planet, to put on paper so that you can understand how life is supposed to be lived and how it can help you in your life.

Before I got into this chapter, I prayed and asked my Creator to give me the wisdom to write and put in this chapter what is in His will and what anyone struggling might need to hear. At the end of the day, there is a Creator—and for me, I found God through Jesus Christ. You can also find God if you search and pray. Plant yourself in a church so that you can heal and get some peace in your mind and soul. In times at church, you will feel peace and nostalgia--a happy childhood feeling that is only from the Creator of heaven and earth. Like the priest told me in the Catholic church, "Where you find God is where you need to be." I will say this: I made it out of the devil's lair and got my life back. And so can you! There is life after alcohol and addiction. Take some time to get into nature, look around, and count the blessings that are currently in your life. Ask God to give you wisdom to get back on track. Maybe you have left your belief, and at one point you did have a relationship and prayed to your higher power. Now is the time to get back and get it right. God never left and will always be there for you when you need Him. In a lifespan, we can see up to 30,000 sunrises—so we do have some time left to get your relationship back and right with God.

The amazing thing is that in my going to church and not going to church, He was always there. The people in my life had all been touched by God, and I believe He also kept me away from the people who were not good for my life. I do believe that once you cross that line and you have a belief— and you witness the goodness of God—He will have a hand in your life and show you how your life can be lived in peace. It does take a surrender to say, "Okay God, help me. What's next? Please get me back on my feet, and I want the Good Life you can promise me."

In the Christian church, there is a prayer of salvation, and in this prayer, you can change your life. It's in the Book of Romans, chapter 10, verse 9. The prayer says, "If you declare with your mouth, 'Jesus is Lord,' and believe in your heart that God raised him from the dead, you will be saved." It was when

I prayed this at the Abundant Church 30 years ago that it changed me. Yes, I was attacked by the evil one, and he wanted to distract me over the years. But I had a purpose, and God had plans for me to write this book and get it out to as many people as I possibly could. What worked for me might not work for you, but it sure is worth trying to change your life and get back on track. While this is not for everyone it was for me, and we need to find some inner peace while we are living and breathing. For some it's playing golf, for some it's going to church. Find you and stick to it. One Day at a Time!

9

30-DAY ALCOHOL BREAK! - THE HARD TRUTH!

STOPPING ALCOHOL FOR 30 DAYS!

The Hard Truth is that we need to stop lying to ourselves and give alcohol a break. It has never been our friend, It's one mission is to kill, steal and destroy your life.

Brandon Lee said:

"Because we don't know when we will die, we get to think of life as an inexhaustible well. And yet everything happens only a certain number of times".

With this quote, I want you to consider that the more you consume alcohol, the more you reduce the number of times you can find joy in your life. Give alcohol a break and see how great your life can become!

In this chapter, I have created a self-help guide to stop drinking alcohol for 30 days. I will guide you with something to look forward to each day. The purpose of these daily coaching tasks is to help you get through each day, and work toward reaching 30 days. The only way it will work is if you commit 110% to it, and follow what we are asking you in each day's affirmation. I am going to say this right now! If you stay in the same mindset of wanting to drink this is not going to work. You are going to need to dig the furthest you have ever dug to stop. You are going to need an Aha moment, something that changes your heart about alcohol. It's been embedded into your subconscious that it's ok to drink. But it's not ok, it's a straight poison that you are putting in your mind and body. To have heart means to have courage and emotion, a deep meaning of stopping. It must be greater than yourself. If you continue to drink the only thing that loses out, is you, no one else. You need a paradigm shift, a fundamental change in how you understand and view sobriety. It's got to involve a move from one way of thinking to a new, a different way to your thoughts. It must result in a significant alteration in how you perceive your reality.

Something I want to also mention is the fact that medication can also help you stop drinking. Looking for a mental help provider that deals with addiction can also help you. I mentioned in previous chapters and just want to mention that medications can help you stop cravings. It will help your mind to get a break. I am not a doctor or physician, but this may help you long term to stop. There are plenty that are non-addictive medications that can help stay away from drinking. One nutrient that helped me was L-Methylfolate or 5-MTHF with B12 with a good multivitamin. It can help the mind with cravings and stabilize mood. It is easy to find online. While it works for some it may not have any effect on others. Another option if you want to take it one step further is to try some

Genetic Testing or Methylation Genetic Testing. This can help you find a nutrition plan to help optimize your recovery or 30-day alcohol-free break on a different level. All this can be found at 10xhealthsystem.com.

One important aspect of each daily affirmation and how to follow it is: don't jump ahead to the next day's reading. Stay focused on your current day and work on that day only. As you read that affirmation for the day, follow the instructions in the order as you read. Don't skip to the end and do what it is asking after you have read it. This is very important so you can grow through each day's affirmation, don't skip around, to get the most benefit from that day's instruction. After your days' affirmation feel free to look at other chapters of the book and learn everything you can about The Hard Truth and Stopping Alcohol.

I also encourage you to get a notebook and every day you will be asked to write down that day's Affirmation. It will be **<u>highlighted and underlined</u>**. Your journal is the key to your success. The writing in your journal is to help you grow each day. In the back of this book, I also have some pages where you can take notes, but I recommend getting a notebook (Journal) to write down your thoughts and ideas as you dive into the affirmations. Also, on certain days, I will ask you to write specific letters to help you get to the end of the 30 days.

Find some Facebook groups to navigate through. These will help you gain insight and answer a lot of questions that you may have on your journey. Some that I recommend are "Alcohol Is Not My Problem Anymore" with Vig Adams or "Sober Sessions" with Joel Anthony. AA and SMART Recovery Facebook groups. Also, make sure to like or follow the Facebook group that is for this book: "The Hard Truth & Stopping Alcohol".

You need to get motivated, and by the end, you will hopefully realize that alcohol just isn't worth it anymore. We are also working to gain a different perspective on alcohol and on yourself. We will learn to dig deep into your thoughts and belief system to help you get a grasp of your drinking. At the end of the 30 days, you will be able to decide if you really want to go back to drinking or continue down a road of sobriety.

If you do go back to drinking, understand that alcohol will again blind you and make you forget all that you learned in the next 30 days. To really grow from the experience, write down all your thoughts in detail so you can go back and look through them each day. This book was designed to help you learn about alcohol and give you resources to help you live a different life without it.

So, let's get this started with Day One. If it's not today, then start early in the morning. Each day, read the affirmation and guide for the day. "You can choose either Day One… or One Day!"

In addition, maybe you're just a weekend drinker and you're working to make it through the week till the weekend to drink. Still, do the daily suggestions and guides and work through them. If alcohol has created problems in your life, like a DWI or possible health issues, now is the time to take a 30-day break. While some will be heavier drinkers than others, the daily guides will take you through 30 days and are designed for moderate to heavy drinkers. Some people take a month or even a few months off. These 30 days are designed to help you decide if you want to quit for good or go back to alcohol use disorder nonsense.

If you're drinking daily to the point of passing out and feel like you drink to stay alive, I recommend getting to an ER or a detox center. Make calls to your local agencies and ask them if they have any room to help you detox from alcohol. Google "detox centers near me." I have heard of people dying from seizures and alcohol withdrawal. It's important to make sure you get some help, and it depends on the severity of your drinking before you start these 30-day affirmations. I am not a doctor or physician and cannot tell you to only relay on this 30-day break. Seeking medical advice before is encouraged and recommended. You also will need to get clearance from your primary care doctor to start these 30 days if you drink more than two to three drinks daily.

So, let's get into it and work to start your transformation and stop for 30 days.

Tomorrow or today is Day One. Read through it and follow it with a clear, positive mindset. Try not to skip to the next day—focus on the day that you are on. Whatever the topic is, write it in your journal and add to it throughout the day. Write down the things you find in your 30-day journey, what challenges you face that day, and include all the positive and negative discoveries you find.

The next day, read what we are to do for that day and keep going until we hit 30 days. Whatever you do—DON'T DRINK. You got this, and LET'S GO!!!!

Remember to go in with positive thoughts about the next 30 days. It can change your life if you are willing to work it and take it seriously. The paradigm shift starts now!

Day One

You must commit 110 % to stopping. There is no in-between. If you're serious about stopping or taking a break, you must want it more than anything in your life right now. Day One is to establish where we are headed on this 30-day journey.

You should have a notebook, or you can use our to-do pages in the back of the book in case you don't have your notebook yet. First, I want you to write down in your journal the 5 most important things in your life right now, in any order. These 5 things need to be what drives you each day. They need to be what matters most in your life right now—what gets you up each day and what you are living for.

After you have written them down, write at the top of the 5: "Stop Drinking Alcohol" in bold, and put a #1 in front underlined. This will help to motivate you to stop for the next 30 days. These should be your reasons for taking an alcohol break for 30 days. Most importantly, do it for yourself, and all these 5 things will flourish from stopping drinking.

It's important to note that this is your journey and your newfound self-respect. Now, get all the alcohol out of the house. All the bottles, all the shot glasses and bottles you may have stashed—put them in a box, dump them, and get rid of them. If you have a collection of bottles, give them away to someone, and that someone shouldn't let you have them in the next 30 days—hopefully for good. Or you can simply just throw them away, which would be the wisest to do.

The saying goes: if you have candy lying around in your house, you're more than likely to have one. Same as the booze —if you have some in the house, time to let it go.

The key to your success is taking one day at a time. Just for today—don't drink. When the time comes that you normally drink, eat a full meal and drink some water—fill your stomach. Make sure you eat three meals today.

<u>Today's Affirmation and In your journal today</u>, I want you to take a personal inventory of your life. Write down all the good things in your life, and all the bad things in your life right now. If you can write 10 good and 10 bad this will help you understand the difference between the two. In addition, write all the bad that alcohol does in your life right now, and how stopping can change this. Do you have any goals in your life? Where do you want to be in the next 5 years? What do you need to do to get to it in 5 years?

Also, write down what stopping alcohol is going to do in your life or what you want it to do for you in the next 30 days. Dig deep and write about these questions throughout the day. Go through the "Why" questions. Why do you Drink? Then dig deep 5 times after that, asking the answer to those questions —"Why?"

If you drink to take away stress, then ask yourself why do you need alcohol to take away stress? Getting to the root cause of why your drinking will help you stop for good. Understanding why you turn to alcohol and drink regularly is important to face head on. Is your mind just needing it to feel normal? What is it, and why do you drink? Getting to the root cause will be key to your success.

Dropping dead weight, like drinking buddies and old hang outs need to happen. Start working to learn as much as you can by educating yourself with books. Also today, I want you to also write down 5 reasons why you think you drink. Work to understand why you drink. What will it take to resolve this issue or issues and seek to resolve your drinking. Get to bed early and wake up to Day Two. If you can't sleep, try to drink some warm milk and eat a banana. If not maybe a sleepy time tea? Work to get to bed at a time you plan to follow for the next 30 days and make this your bedtime. You Got This! One Day at a time! Acronym is ODAAT.

Day 2

This day has a new sense of attitude and remember—you must want this. You made it 24 hours, now it's time to do it again. The saying goes: one day at a time. Just for today, don't drink.

<u>Today Affirmation</u> - in your journal, I want you to write a letter to yourself—write it to you as your best friend. Dig deep and write a letter about why you want to stop for 30 days. Keep this letter with you today and for the next few days or weeks. Look deep into yourself and write why you want to stop drinking. Why and how stopping for 30 days is going to benefit you?

If you were to write to your best friend, what encouragement would you give them? Try to get emotional about this letter and give it meaning. Create Heart in this letter which means Courage and emotion. In this letter, I want you to include the bad things alcohol has done to you personally, and to your family. Another thing I want you to write about is why you don't need to drink. Add, I don't need to drink because? Dig deep into this, because it can help you realize that you don't really need it. Put as much detail in this letter as you can, the more you elaborate the more it will help you.

Eat three solid meals today, drink plenty of water and hydrate, take a vitamin. Try to get some exercise today—even if it's a run or a brisk walk.

Something that has helped people with cravings are the next items—I don't recommend a lot of sweets, but some can help:

- Candy
- Ice cream
- Chocolate
- Fizzy drink
- Eat a big meal
- Find a meditation class
- YouTube meditation
- Manual labor
- Physical activity
- Exercise
- Yell at yourself to stop
- Sugary foods (do you have a candy bar you like? Get one today)

The sugary foods are not recommended on a daily basis, and can affect your blood sugar levels and mental states. As an Alcoholic and drinking regularly, we have witnessed malnutrition. Working now to eat three meals a day and healthy snacking is going to be crucial for the next 30 days. Snacks could include – raw vegetables, nuts, wheat crackers and cheese in a sandwich bag. Google the USDA three meals a day plan--it can help. Also, the USDA Food and Nutrition page has a lot of information to look at.

Alcohol would release dopamine, and we need to release some today. As we have always been told don't make sweets a habit—in the beginning, but it can help. But exercise is a much healthier way to release the dopamine your mind will be craving. A hot shower, sometimes an allergy pill like Benadryl (not recommended daily—some have gotten dependent on it) for a temporary chill moment, can help you sleep. A lot of times we can't sleep, and it is totally normal. Some good sleepy teas or melatonin can help. Melatonin isn't for everyone, so best to give it a try.

If it doesn't work, try something else. Magnesium oxide is a supplement that can help for sleep also. If it gets to the point where you can't sleep at all, go to your health care provider and see if they can prescribe something. Also work to meet with your general practitioner and see if they can help.

Again, a sleepy tea can help if you haven't tried it already. Some will have a hard time sleeping, others may want to sleep more than normal. This is ok as your body is healing and could need the extra sleep. Creating a routine and sleep pattern is crucial in the beginning. Do an online meeting sometime today. Here is the website link: http://aa-intergroup.org/ —it's at the top of the hour, every hour. Just be an observer. You don't have to participate—just listen.

Read your notes today and work to get some rest for Day 3.

Day 3

Keep in mind you're fresh from stopping drinking and if you're not feeling well this is not what sobriety feels like, this is what detoxing from a poison feels like. This is the day that you really need to see how you are feeling. On the third day, the alcohol has left the building. If you have the shakes or have a serious headache, it's time to get to a doctor and see if they can help with the withdrawal. I am not a doctor and can't recommend medication. But remember—if you're not feeling right, you need to get some help. Make the calls.

I have included in this book, in Chapter 3, several numbers for people to call if you experience any alcohol withdrawal. You could simply get to a hospital and ask to be evaluated. There are detox locations you can call to see if they have any openings. If you're craving or just don't feel right, get some help—but whatever you do, don't drink. We are committed to stopping, and let's stick to it. Fight the good fight. You are 72 hours in, and the alcohol has left your body. The mind will make you think you want it, but you don't need it. It's been embedded subconsciously, and you need to understand that you don't need it.

It all depends on how much you drank, but if you were a moderate drinker, then you will be okay with the recommendations in Day 2 for cravings. If you're a heavy drinker, withdrawal can cause seizures or life-threatening complications—it's best to get some help with your detox. Some need to go to inpatient care and get medication through it.

Today, I want you to get into another meeting online if you can. Search AA and find a meeting. Again, Chapter 3 will give you the tools to find an AA Group. Google it or download the app—it's a blue circle with a white chair in it ("Meeting Guide")—to your phone for local meetings. Online meetings: http://aa-intergroup.org/. This is a link to meetings every hour on the hour.

Today try to do some exercise—go for a run or walk. Eat three meals and hydrate. hydrate, hydrate to detox all the toxins.

Today is a good day to start with some prayers, prayers that you feel comfortable with and remember to take it one day at a time.

Today's Affirmation in your journal - I want you to take a personal inventory of yourself. Ask yourself deep questions like:

- What are my strengths?
- Where do I need improvement? (Career, relationships, health, spirituality, finances, fun).
- What other fun can you do besides drinking? (Waking up feeling like crap from drinking isn't fun) Old hobbies or activities that doesn't involve drinking.

Reflect on past successes and failures to see patterns in your life. Take today to make a personal inventory of yourself and your life.

Also, write down how you are feeling today and record it in your journal.

Remember to keep eating three meals and work to make it another 24 hours. Try not to eat everything in sight—just a good three meals (breakfast, lunch, and dinner).

Day 4

If we made it to this day, we are truly committed and want this more than anything. If you're not withdrawing and are doing okay, we are going to make it another day of no alcohol. Remember to eat your three meals today. Start working toward healthy eating—something that is good for you and won't put on the pounds. What do you like that is somewhat healthy? Get this going in your life.

If you can, start working on the 12 steps from AA—I highly recommend giving them a try. While it's not for everyone it has helped millions recover and stop. It's worth looking into it. There is also SMART recovery online, It's limited to regions and what groups are available. The website to check for your area is - www.smartrecovery.org . Top right is a meeting finder, to find a meeting open up the distance and push the + to get a greater distance. You can go up to 1000 miles if you would like to. They also have a 4-point SMART recovery handbook that you can order on the website. On the website there is also a tab for personal support. There are also Facebook groups for Smart Recovery called SMART Recovery works – or another is SMART recovery tools & Philosophy.

This is the day I am going to tell you: if you want to go to a facility to see how they can help you or make some calls and set up an appointment, then follow up. Outpatient programs or substance abuse counseling can help. Make the calls and see what you can do.

We need to start avoiding people, places, and things that give us triggers to drink. People we would go drinking with, places we would go and drink or meet with friends, things that make us want to drink must be avoided.

Maybe going to a game or hearing live music would make you want to drink—avoid them for these 30 days. If you absolutely must go, have a plan for what you will do if you want to drink, and stick to it. Maybe a nonalcoholic drink or a mocktail. There are some you can order online. I haven't tried all of them but have tried one or two of them. Here are some of the names you can try - Recess, Moment, Peak Cocktails, Tru Kava. For some, it's a slippery slope—and if it is, stay away from it. You know yourself. Be careful about the infused THC ones that defeat the purpose of having a sober drink other than alcohol. While some do use CBD or THC infused, we are not working to empower the use. If you choose that's your journey and life, right now we are focusing on being alcohol free. Do what's going to help you stop for these 30 days. They do have some of the fizzy nonalcoholic drinks at your local health store as well.

We can work on practicing what to say if someone asks why you're not drinking. You can say, "I'm taking a break for 30 days," or "My liver needs a break." Whatever you feel good saying and whatever works for you.

If sleep is still messing with you, you might want to talk to a doctor or go to a pharmacy to see what they might have to help. Some options:

- Benadryl (not recommended daily)
- Valerian root tea (like extra sleepy time tea) There are different ones at health food stores like Sprouts, Whole Foods, local grocery stores, Walgreens.
- Chamomile tea
- Magnesium Glycinate is a good supplement to help with sleep.

Start Creating a routine for yourself. Create a bedtime that will work for you to get to bed each night. Breathing exercises will help get oxygen in the blood. Taking a hot shower will help release melatonin. Find what works for you and create a routine that makes sense.

You can also Google "things to help me sleep" and see

what might work for you. Try to stop at a health food store and work to see what sleep aids you can find.

<u>Today's affirmation</u>: in your journal, I want you to write down how messed up drinking can make you. Maybe you have it under control, maybe you don't. But write down the stupid stuff you have done in the past—and why you shouldn't do it again. Maybe you feel it wasn't that bad, and you were a good person when you drank, write down anything on the negative aspects of alcohol that you can think. Write down all the negative results you experience from drinking. Hangover? Hangxiety? Headaches? Whatever it is write it down.

Focus on this today and put as many thoughts as possible in your journal about your past drinking. This is between you and yourself. Nobody else. So be brutally honest with yourself in this lesson. Take your time and dig deep to discover all the negative outcomes alcohol has caused you in your life.

Day 5

Today I want you to realize that you've made it almost a week, and it's usually these days that are the most tempting—so you must keep fighting to stay sober, just for today. Weekends are especially harder if you're used to drinking on weekends. What has worked for you over the past 4 days? Keep this in mind and keep it going if it's working. Start changing your thoughts about alcohol. Start telling yourself I don't need it. Early I started creating a hate for the ads and posters I would see. The companies working to add to their billions through marketing.

Today, say a prayer and/or plan on going to church, or possibly call a friend who doesn't drink have a conversation with them. Maybe, ask them what church they go to. Maybe reach out to a family member who goes to church. If there's a church you've been thinking about trying, give it a try. Get out of your comfort zone - it's all about change and trying something new. Reframing your thoughts is key to growing out of the addiction.

If today isn't a typical church day like Wednesday or Sunday, then plan to go sometime this week and hear the message. If you don't want to go to church, then don't—but do an AA meeting online or in person. The reason for an AA meeting or getting to a church is to try new things in your life. Maybe going to church is not for you currently. Then adventure out or get into something that you have not done yet. Listening to an AA meeting online gives some perspective on what others go through in their journey to stopping drinking. Do a Smart meeting, remember stopping is possible at any point of your drinking career. The long-term results of drinking are going to be lingering. So, remember, the longer you stayed on that wrong ride, the more expensive it's going to be to get home.

Remember, it's 30 days. You got this.

<u>Today in your journal</u>, write a letter to alcohol. Tell it all the things you've wanted to say that you never have. We need to start creating resentment toward alcohol, it was never your friend.

Remember, we are focusing on 30 days with no booze—but really, it's just for today. Keep your journal with you throughout the day. Add to it as something comes to your mind that you would like to add. It will be your safety net and a reminder of what you are working to accomplish in this 30 days alcohol break. ODAAT (one day at a time).

Day 6

Wake up and thank God, you made it another day! Start realizing how better you feel when waking up, not hung over or feeling the after effects of the poison. Today, I want you to think of things you used to do for fun as a teenager or even a young adult. Start caring about yourself more. Go get a haircut, and if you can, buy some new clothes. One thing you will find is that you start to revert to your true self when stopping alcohol.

When you start to think of some fun things you did as your younger self, why not give them a try? Or, if there's something you have been wanting to do, let's give that a try—drawing, playing guitar, dribbling a soccer ball, tennis, running, going to the gym, cooking, gardening, hiking, mountain biking, skateboarding, rollerblading.

Think about some new hobbies you want to get into. Look into them and give them a try. Whatever has been working for you over the past six days, do it again. Remember to eat three meals, take some vitamins, and hydrate.

<u>Today in your journal</u>, write down some things that interest you. Maybe something you have done in the past, see if you can work to get back into them. Also, write down interests you have in mind and what they can and will make you feel. Gardening, color books, something different you can try. Also write about the benefits of trying something new, and what that will bring to your life.

If you can't think of anything, watch a good sober movie. Google "sober movies" and find one that interests you today. Find an audible book for sobriety. A podcast on sobriety. YouTube a sober podcast.

Day 7

Take it slow today. In your journal, write what you have discovered over the past 7 days, good and bad. Write down any struggles you may have had and how you made it through them. What were the highlights and triumphs? What would you do differently? What are you going to plan to do in the next 7 days?

You made it one week, and this is probably a huge accomplishment. Maybe you have been sober and doing this, or not—but the writings in your journal are the reasons you are keeping on this 30-day affirmation to stop.

Get an iced tea with extra ice (or no ice), a soda, apple juice, or something nonalcoholic and toast yourself. Say, "You made it 7 days, and I am proud of you." Now let's make it another 23 days.

<u>Today's journal affirmation</u> I want you to write about any triggers you may have had to create awareness of them. Also, write what you want to get out of the rest of your 23 days not drinking. Make a list of 5 positive affirmations you want to accomplish from the next weeks and days ahead. Is there anything specific you want to work on in these 30 days? Some examples of positive affirmations are:

- Start reading a book that interests you
- Get to 3 AA meetings this week
- Start eating healthier / Make time for 3 meals a day
- Get to bed Earlier
- Get some yard work done
- It can be anything that has a positive emotion

These will be important for you're the next 23 days to help you reach your goal.

Keep doing what has been working for you so far. Be positive, positivity starts with in. Working to create a positive mental attitude, a mindset that helps you to reprogram your mind. If something negative pops into your mind, try to change it to a positive thought. The triggers you wrote in your journal, what is your plan to not let them lead you to drink? Having a plan is important while wanting to stay away from drinking. Have your plan and commit to it.

Day 8

Today, try this: If it's after work, change and go somewhere outdoors. If you think of the park, go to the park. If it's too cold, take a drive and sit in your car at the park. If you have a family, ask them to give you one hour to just take a minute to yourself.

<u>Take your journal and write down some happy thoughts</u> —thoughts that don't involve drinking and that make you happy. You know you. Talk to your inner self and find what makes you happy! These are important, and you must find more of this.

If you can't go to a park, sit in your room for a little bit, somewhere you can sit and be alone and write in your journal - ask yourself what makes you happy?

These things that make you happy are important, and you need to focus on them daily for the rest of these days. If there is one that stands out, embrace it and try to do more of this. We are working on changing our thought patterns. Trying to create new thoughts in our minds will help us break the alcohol chains.

Keep trying to attend an AA meeting, or Smart Meeting, either in person or online. Make sure you're eating your meals and taking your vitamins.

The reason for this exercise is to understand that life does have some happy moments, and we don't need alcohol to have a happy moment.

Day 9

Today when you wake up, I want you to stretch. Do a variety of stretches that you would do before any activity, maybe some that you did when you were in elementary school. With stretching, take some deep breaths and/or count to 10 while holding each position. Getting a good leg stretch in, back stretches are a good way to help release lower back tension.

Start noticing how clear your thoughts are becoming.

<u>Today, write in your journal</u> Some good memories you had as a child. Maybe your early teen years. Just write down good memories you had before you ever picked up a drink. Also, in your journal write a bucket list. Places you want to go, or things you want to try. In the next 5 years, work to get a couple of them done. The point of this is to make you realize that there was a time that you did not drink and we don't need to drink to live or enjoy life. The mind already knows how to work without alcohol. The mind is resilient, and you can go back to that mindset. How do you do this, the longer you stay away from alcohol.

Also, if you have any exercise equipment, get some of that in for 30 minutes. If you must get to work, then do something short—like 3 sets of 10 jumping jacks. Do some running in place for 30 seconds to a minute. The goal is to get the heart rate up and release some dopamine early in the morning. We can have coffee or tea after—or before—whatever works for you.

Work to get a meeting in, but whatever you do, make it another 21. You got this. One day at a time.

Today, think of exercise as an outlet. Write in your journal some goals you want to try. Maybe a new workout? Maybe a gym? Maybe work to get a good hike today. Write a goal you want to try for the remaining days in this 30-day journey and make it a routine. Have a park near you? Go for a walk, or find a hiking trail and get a mile in.

Day 10

We are at a point in this 30-day sober journey where we need to start asking ourselves how we are doing. We need to talk to ourselves. Some people may think it's a little weird, but it's good to talk to yourself.

Let's try a motivation speech! Talk to yourself and tell yourself all the good things you have accomplished in the past 10 days. Look in the mirror and give yourself a high 5. **For this day's exercise** we are going to have a chat with our inner self. Work to talk to your inner self and get a motivating speech going. If you find it strange to talk to yourself then write it in your journal. Here is a motivational speech example – The power of One Step.

Today, I want to talk to you about the power of **one step**. Just one.

It's easy to feel overwhelmed by the distance between

where you are and where you want to be. Goals can seem too big. Dreams can feel far away. Obstacles can look impossible to move. But here's The Hard Truth: you don't climb a mountain by leaping to the top. You get there **one step at a time**.

Every great achievement, every invention, every breakthrough, every success story—began with someone who dared to take a step. Not a giant leap. Not a perfect plan. Just a single step forward.

You don't have to have it all figured out. You just have to move. Make the call. Show up. Try. Fail. Learn. Try again. Because **progress isn't about perfection, it's about persistence**.

There will be setbacks. There will be days you want to quit. But in those moments, remind yourself: you've made it through every challenge life has thrown at you so far. You're stronger than you think. You're braver than you believe. And you're more capable than you know.

So take the step. Don't wait for permission. Don't wait for the perfect time. You have everything you need to begin— right now.

Because one step can change your direction. One step can build your momentum. And one step… can change your life.

In your Journal write down what your motivational speech would be. Think about it and take it to heart. Make it the most promising and uplifting speech you have ever heard. Keep your journal with you today and add to this speech through the day.

Today, don't drink. Get a good workout in—push the limit. This workout will help you release the dopamine that has been messed with during your alcohol use.

Day 11

Today I want to work to Learn a little more about AA or Smart Recovery. I understand that AA is not for everyone, and don't limit yourself to having to give only AA a try. You can also look into SMART Recovery at smartrecovery.org, SMART Recovery is the leading, evidence-informed approach to overcoming addictive behaviors and leading a balanced life. SMART Recovery is stigma-free and emphasizes self-empowerment. They have a handbook called the 4- point program handbook, and a mobile app for access to meetings, tools, and help manage urges. If you do SMART Recovery, I recommend for the 30 Days to abstain from Alcohol although they say SMART doesn't require abstinence we are stopping for these 30 days and working to stop for good.

AA was created to stop drinking long-term and for good. If you can Look into getting an AA book through Amazon or go to Barnes & Noble (I have listed the 12 steps below if you don't have an AA book). You can also find some other books at Barnes & Noble to help stop drinking. The more education you can get the better as you grow in this alcohol free journey. Knowledge is power and the more you educate yourself the better you can work to stop completely. Go back into the chapters of this book and read on the hijack and really learn all you can. Another book was Alcohol Explained by William Porter that really gave me insight to learn more about what I was putting into my mind and body. It's available on Amazon and audible as well. You can also find some pages just by Googling the Alcoholics Anonymous book. Sometimes, if you go to a meeting, they have some books they can give you.

Look over the 12 steps, and in your journal this day, write

down one step that speaks to you the most. Once you have that step written down, think about it and begin to break it down. Study it, look it up online, and gather your thoughts about what it means to you. If you want to explore any other of the steps or all of them, I recommend indulging and learning all that you can. Write down any details that speak out to you, and what you learn about it in your journal.

If you think SMART Recovery is a better approach for you then look it up and see what you can learn about it. Order the 4-Point PROGRAM HANDBOOK and implement the tools the handbook offers. Some find a better sober life by getting involved in their church. Some become more involved in their personal hobbies and create routines that keep them from drinking. Whatever works for you stick to it each day. Create routine and habit. AA and SMART recovery are tools and just a guide to help you get to your 30 days with no booze. It also gives us a perspective of how AA and SMART Recovery help others. So being open and learning helps us understand that there is help, and there are people willing to help you make it to a better life without alcohol if we need it.

There is a movie about Bill Wilson, the founder of AA, that was interesting. It has a lot of drinking in it, so I recommend being cautious. Also, *The Lois Wilson Story*, which is called *When Love Is Not Enough*. I recommend seeing that one before you see *The Bill Wilson Story*. It was interesting to see both perspectives of the two movies. One was his wife's perspective, and the other was through his eyes. Mr. Wilson passed in 1971, and Alcoholics Anonymous is one of the strongest fellowships to date for stopping alcohol. It's about being there for each other and standing with each other to be clean and sober, and to also work to help others who are in alcohol use disorder. While helping others, we help ourselves.

By going to a meeting, you can find a sponsor to call if you need help. For right now, keep looking into AA and Smart Recovery and dig into one for **this day's affirmation. Write In your Journal** what you have learned about AA or Smart recovery that interests you. Or anything that you have learned from looking into them. Get a online AA meeting today or tonight http://aa-intergroup.org/. If you have a craving, get in an online meeting. It's every hour on the hour.

The 12 steps:

1. We admitted we were powerless over alcohol, that our lives had become unmanageable. Get into Facebook groups and ask a question about your sobriety.
2. Came to believe that a Power greater than ourselves could restore us to sanity.
3. Made a decision to turn our will and our lives over to the care of God as we understood Him.
4. Made a searching and fearless moral inventory of ourselves.
5. Admitted to God, to ourselves, and to another human being the exact nature of our wrongs.
6. Were entirely ready to have God remove all these defects of character.
7. Humbly asked Him to remove our shortcomings.
8. Made a list of all the people we had harmed and became willing to make amends to them all.
9. Made direct amends to such people wherever

possible, except when to do so would injure them or others.

10. Continued to take personal inventory and when we were wrong, promptly admitted it.

11. Sought through prayer and meditation to improve our conscious contact with God as we understood Him, praying only for knowledge of His will for us and the power to carry that out.

12. Having had a spiritual awakening as the result of these Steps, we tried to carry this message to alcoholics and to practice these principles in all our affairs.

Day 12

Today I want you to Google and learn about alcohol. Discover the things that no one ever talks about. Google "World Health Organization and alcohol-related deaths." Start learning what alcohol does to your body and your mind. Google information like how female consumption of alcohol is related to cancers. If you want to ask some questions and really break things down, you can learn some interesting facts. Go to chapgpt.com, sign in, and start asking away.

I want this day to be about really researching alcohol and learning as much as you can about it. What diseases can alcohol cause? How does alcohol affect the brain and white matter in the brain? How does alcohol get into your cells? What does alcohol do to the body and mind? What part of the brain does alcohol affect?

In your Journal I want you to write everything that you discovered. Try to add to it throughout the day, and if you even think about drinking, look at these answers and say, "Just not for today." You are thriving right now, and your mind is finally getting a break from alcohol. Your body and mind appreciate you.

Let's go for another 24 hours. You got this.

Day 13

Today, talk with a close friend or family member about what you have learned so far in your journey and what you think about being alcohol free for 13 Days. Find one person you want to talk to and simply ask them, "Do you know what alcohol does to the body and mind?" See what they tell you. Then, go into your notes, look up what you learned yesterday and talk to them about it.

Go over the details of what alcohol does to so many people and what never really gets talked about. **<u>Write in your Journal today</u>** what you all discussed in the conversation.

Day 14

Today is a new day, and we are almost halfway through your 30-day, no-alcohol journey. As we are further into our journey of 14 day's we need to start realizing all the years, months or days you have drank. It's going to take time to feel and become your true self. As we are growing, we also need to have some self-respect for yourself and respect for others. **<u>In your journal today</u>,** I want you to write down all the people you have harmed through your drinking. Maybe it was someone you told off, or an old friend you talked smack to—make a list. You may feel they deserved it. But also, the frontal lobe of your decision-making areas of the brain gets suppressed with alcohol, and we will act without rationalizing the action. Alcohol has and will get us in more trouble as we continue drinking.

In AA, this is step 9 of their 12 steps. But with this list, I want you to focus on seeing who you have harmed because of alcohol—anyone you spoke to in a rude or indecent way. The saying goes: *treat people the way you want to be treated.* Maybe you had your reasons, but the fact is, you were not in your right mind.

Now that you have your list, I want you to pick one person you feel comfortable talking to and apologize for what you said or did. This will open a whole new version of yourself and help you begin to take accountability for your actions and what alcohol has done to your relationships.

Write in your journal Go to a meeting AA or SMART, and this time, share in the meeting—see how it makes you feel. Write down how it made you feel and what you experienced.

Make it another 24 hours. One day at a time.

Day 15

Halfway done with your 30 day no-alcohol journey!

Today, look through your journal and reflect on the past 15 days. See all the positive things you've experienced from not drinking and what stood out to you—write this in your journal. Really take time to reflect on everything you've gone through so far and take it all in. Feel it. Acknowledge your growth and begin thinking about what the next 15 days will look like in this journey.

In your journal today, write down what you want to accomplish in the next 15 days. Start setting goals for yourself. Maybe one goal could be starting an old sport you used to enjoy. Or visit a gym in your area, walk around, and consider signing up with a trainer. Thought about Cross Fit? Google some locations near you and go check one out.

Start working to set positive, reinforcing goals for yourself. Maybe one goal is to lose some weight—write down what it would take to make it happen. For any goals you might have, also write down the obstacles that could prevent you from starting or achieving them, and how you can work to overcome those challenges.

Today, eat a good dinner—and whatever you do, don't drink. Put your goal and your plan into action. It doesn't have to be a physical activity you can also try other non-active new Hobbie goals.

Here are some ideas to try:

- Take an online course
- Try painting—find a creative outlet
- Find some coloring books
- Puzzles can help when working to clear the mind
- Do some work outside in the yard, Gardening is an outlet (have a goal to plant a small garden)
- Pick up an instrument you've always wanted to play
- Volunteer at your local church or a homeless shelter

Day 16

Today, rearrange your room. If you don't want to rearrange your room, get rid of some old clothes that you never wear and take them to Goodwill. Move the paintings on your walls around—rearrange them. Put some in new places and get rid of the ones that are old you don't want anymore. Take them to Goodwill, give them to a friend, and work on getting some new ones put up.

The point of this is to start reprogramming your mind. It's important because you want to begin thinking differently. Our thoughts create triggers, and we think we want to drink—for a reward, or to relieve the stress that happened during the day. Learning to think differently is important when breaking free from alcohol.

In the morning, make sure to start making your bed if you don't already, it will help clear your mind and get you ready for the day.

Today, I want you to maybe try a non-alcoholic drink. Also, there are things in the market that are used to help relax. Drinks like GUINEP, Juni, Recess, U-relax, Moment, Hiyo are botanical adaptogens sodas that can help. They can be found at sprouts or other stores like Target and online. This can be a slippery slope for some. Also, if they make you feel off or not right, then don't drink them. If you think it will make you want the real thing, then don't consider it. For me, I tried a couple, and I can see them as a good alternative to not drinking alcohol. The point is you don't need a drink that contains any poison- and that's what alcohol is. It is poison. Alcohol is a delusion, hiding what it's really about. Drinking is only going to make you feel like crap later.

Also, if you ever drink during this process of stopping, you have to start over. So don't have an alcoholic drink today.

Let's go for another 24 hours.

In your journal today., I want you to write down: "What makes you me happy?" In Day 8 we wrote down thoughts that make you happy.

Today I want you to write what are the things that truly make your life better and bring you happiness? (Alcohol cannot be one of them.) The things in your life that make you happy start today and learn to be grateful for the things that bring happiness into your life. These Things that bring you happiness are reasons not to be drinking today and in the next couple weeks ahead.

Also write down: "What values are most important to me?" Some Core value examples include beauty, honesty, discipline, truth, responsibility, and kindness.

When you write down a core value that is important to you, why is it important to you? If you don't have any or would like to bring more into your life. Write down which core values you can start implementing in your life.

Day 17

Today, let's look into your future. The past is the past, but the future holds many positive possibilities.

Let's talk about your bucket list. Do you have one? What are some things you want to do in your life before you pass on?

Today, write a letter to your future self. Write about where you are now and what you want to achieve. In a second paragraph, write to your younger self. Give them advice and encouragement about what to look out for. Tell your younger self what alcohol has done in your life and what you hope they avoid with alcohol in the future.

The purpose of this day—and this letter—is to open your

eyes to what alcohol has done in your life, and what you could have avoided by not drinking. Write as much as you can in this letter. Take time today to add to it throughout the day. Work to learn from this letter and implement them into your life.

Day 18

Wake up and thank God for another day to be alive.

Today in your journal think, gather your thoughts and write about something that happened while drinking that was negative. Write down all the negative results you have had because of drinking. Write down all the times you lost your keys (do you remember?). Have you lost your wallet? How many times can you remember getting home, falling asleep, and then having to check your bank account to see how much money you spent? Did you ever drive drunk? What could have been the long-term effects if you had crashed or gotten a DWI? Write the answers in your journal.

Try to write down all the things alcohol has done to you—those frustrating, forgotten moments you didn't want to remember.

The purpose of this lesson and writing exercise is to really open your mind to what alcohol really does to our judgment. We have to realize that alcohol restricts the function of our frontal lobe, which is responsible for decision-making. The damage that alcohol has caused to your mind is done, but we can work to change that and salvage what we can.

You need to start realizing that bars and alcohol companies don't care what alcohol has done—or will do—to you. They don't care what you will do to yourself. As long as you're contributing to their billion-dollar industry, you are caught in their trap.

By this day, we should start feeling better. Our minds are clearer, and we can make rational decisions for ourselves and our families.

Day 19

<u>Today is the day we should write down</u> triggers that spark the thought to possibly drink. If someone gets you upset, that is a trigger. If you have a bad day, holidays, events are all triggers to drink. Before, we would include alcohol in just about everything we do. It was always a part of the activity.

Now that we have stopped for these 18 days, let's write down in our journal, what our triggers might be. Write down the ones we don't expect, and how you plan to make it through if they arise. Write down all the future and past triggers you will have had or might have.

Next to each trigger write down how you should handle them—or did handle them. Write down, if you are in a situation and you feel uncomfortable, what you are going to do. Talk to your loved ones and let them know: if this happens, I am going to leave; or if I feel uncomfortable, I am going to leave.

One of the biggest conversations is: What do I do with an event or gathering that has alcohol? Or when are you going to be around friends or family that drink? What do you tell them? If you want to take a mocktail or one of the drinks I mentioned in a previous in day 16.

Here are some points that can help. Simply say, "I am taking a break right now." "I get an allergy." "I got a headache." Or "I am tired; it will just make me more tired."

You can say whatever feels right to you. But the key is to have something you want to say if that situation comes up. This is what I say: "My liver can't take it anymore. I went pro at an early age and retired early." "Oh, and did you know alcohol kills 3 million people every year? I didn't know that. "No, I am good, thanks."

You are almost 10 days away from your 30-day goal. You got this far —now keep going and work to get to an online meeting today. They are every hour on the hour. http://aa-inter group.org/ Then just click online meetings.

Day 20

What has been the most rewarding thing you have experienced so far from not drinking? Write down what you have liked so far about not drinking and what you are getting out of it. It could be as simple as not waking up with a hangover or being glad that you can remember what happened the night before.

Let's keep it on a positive note and write down what you have gotten out of time not drinking.

Then I also want you to write down what has been the most challenging thing so far in the past 20 days.

You only have 10 more days to go—and a lifetime ahead of you.

In your journal, write down as many positive things as you have found by not drinking. Take this day to write down as many as you can. These are all reasons not to drink today—or ever. We are on this 30-day break to analyze our relationship with alcohol and really determine if we really need it in our life. The positive things you have discovered by not drinking alcohol are only going to grow and enlighten your life even more. Stay positive and work to keep this positive mindset. Remember Alcohol is a brain disease and the sooner we start reprogramming our thoughts the more we can learn to distance ourselves from alcohol. We need to start having the thoughts I make it this far without alcohol do I really need this in my life? No, you really don't. Let's keep taking it one day at a time.

Day 21

What is success? The predictable result of hard work, patience, sacrifice, and learning put into practice every day. This applies to anything in life.

But are you putting in the hard work these days—not drinking and stopping the booze? Break it down one day at a time. Write down in your journal: "What is the true meaning of one day at a time?"

In one day, you have 24 hours. That's 1,440 Minutes in 24 hours. Sometimes, when we stop drinking, we have to go minute by minute, second by second.

Take the time right now to stop and listen to your heart beating. Take 15 seconds to feel your heart in your chest. Feel your mind connected with your heartbeat. You're alive and strong—and you have a lot of time left in your life.

Take some deep breaths and try to relax your mind. Breathe in through your nose and out through your mouth. Take a deep breath in through your nose… and out through your mouth. With every breath, feel all your stress leaving your body. These are meditation techniques that can help you when you have a craving. But most of all, they help you understand that some-times we need to live in the moment—not for tomorrow, not for what has happened, but for the right here and now.

Put on the song *Right Now* by Van Halen. Go to YouTube and type in Van Halen – Right Now (Lyrics HD). Read the lyrics and take in what that song really means.

<u>Write in your journal</u> the true meaning of Right Now! It's your Tomorrow! Catch that magic moment! Turn this thing around! Write down what it means to live in the moment when stopping alcohol.

What is the meaning of right now in your life and can you take some time to just live in the moment. We need to take this day and work to just live in the moment.

Day 22

The art of letting go.

Now that we can work to live in the moment—at the top of a piece of paper, write down "struggles!" because on this paper, we are going to write down the struggles that we have had. Write down all the struggles you have faced up until today while being sober—struggles with work, family, trying to stay sober. Write it in detail and put it all on that paper. We want to work on learning how to put things on paper. The reason we keep a journal is to help us remember, but to also release it on paper.

Now, on a separate piece of paper, I want you to write about some heavy luggage that has happened in your life and has weighed on you. Whatever that is, write it down and how it affected you. Once you've written everything down, take a moment to look and go through each one. Think about the feelings these struggles caused. Try to isolate them and categorize them in your mind. Visualize them placed inside a box.

Now, get some matches or a lighter. Go outside—or maybe

take a hike if you prefer. Find a designated area that is safe for small flames. Light the paper on fire. As the flames burn all the struggles and heavy luggage, let them go. That box in your mind where they were stored—see it opening. See the feelings leaving your mind. Visualize them disappearing as the paper burns, imagine those burdens leaving your life for good.

This is a powerful way to start fresh and let all the luggage in your life go. Feel the reward of letting them go for good.

<u>Write down in your journal</u> what you felt and experienced from this exercise.

Day 23

Seven more days until it's 30 days with no booze.

On this day, I want you to start the day with tea, coffee, or whatever you drink in the morning—even a nice cold bottle of water. **<u>And for today's journal</u>**- I want you to write down the thing's alcohol has stolen, killed, and destroyed in your life over the years. Write down what it has stolen – For example: money, time, energy. Anything that comes to mind. Waking up at 2 p.m. hungover, is a time thief for sure!

Write down what alcohol has killed – What relationships has alcohol killed over the years?

Write down what it has destroyed – What has alcohol destroyed? Marriages? Jobs? Careers? Put them all down.

I mentioned earlier in the chapter about 1 Peter 5:8 - 9, which is also on the back cover of this book—because your adversary on this earth is out to steal, kill, and destroy. And what does alcohol do? Just that.

It's not your friend, and you need to see all the enjoyment it has destroyed in your life. Once this is on paper and you see it, make sure that you realize that it's not meant for any good on this planet. Its main purpose is to eliminate all the blessings in your life. I mentioned this several times in the book. It kills 3 Million people each year. This is according to the World Health Organization.

Day 24

Dive into number 24.

You will hear this a lot: Make it another 24 Hours. Twenty-four hours a day. The first AA chip has a 24 on it. It's all about focusing on one day at a time.

In the next 24 hours, I want you to reflect on what role everyone plays in your life and what meaning they bring to it. Sit down with your significant other or close friend and discuss what each of you means to the other. Everything lives and dies, yet we never consider this. Today let's talk to them about what they mean to us. There are times when someone passes, and we wish we had said or done something. Tomorrow is not guaranteed, and we need to value the presence of the living. Tell them while they are alive.

<u>Also, in your journal, write a message</u> to someone who has passed—someone you wanted to say something that you couldn't. It can be anyone. If there is more than one person, write to them also. This can help open your heart when you talk to your spouse or any loved one you want to connect with. Let them know how much you value them in your life—and why.

Day 25

Turn a negative situation into a positive one. How? First, don't let the enemy have a seat at your table.

There are going to be times when you want to have a drink, or your mind is not right, and it crosses your mind to have a drink. That's part of the hijack—what is embedded in your mind from years of drinking. The saying goes: you create the first drink in your mind before you even drink.

Here are some steps that can help you avoid losing the last 25 days—or all your sober days—by giving in and having a drink. Know that it will only take you back to where you started. A lot of times, you go back even worse than before.

Here are **10 ways to turn a negative situation into a positive one**:

1. **Reframe the Perspective**
   - Instead of focusing on what went wrong, ask yourself, "What can I learn from this?"—and don't go have a drink.
   - Look for the hidden lesson or opportunity for growth in the situation.
2. **Practice Gratitude**
   - Find at least one thing to be grateful for, even in a tough situation.
   - Gratitude shifts your mindset and helps you focus on the positive.
3. **Control What You Can, Let Go of What You Can't**
   - Focus on the actions and mindset you can

control rather than stressing over things beyond your reach.

- Focus on how far you have come in just 25 days.

4. **Turn It into a Learning Experience**
   - Mistakes and setbacks can be valuable teachers.
   - Analyze what happened and use the experience to avoid similar issues in the future.

5. **Use Humor to Lighten the Mood**
   - Find something funny about the situation, laughter reduces stress and provides perspective.
   - A good sense of humor helps you bounce back faster.

6. **Help Others Going Through Similar Situations**
   - Turn your struggles into an opportunity to support and encourage someone else.
   - Helping others can boost your own mood and give your sobriety a sense of purpose. Remember, it's your journey—do not push sobriety on anyone.

7. **Take a Break and Step Back**
   - Distance yourself from the situation for a while. This is a good tool to avoid doing something you can't erase. Walk away or just leave. Count to 1 backwards from 5,4,3,2,1. Work to have a different thought.
   - A fresh perspective can help you see solutions and possibilities you might have missed.

8. **Surround Yourself with Positivity**
   - Engage with uplifting people, books, or activities that reinforce an optimistic outlook.

- ○ Avoid negativity and toxic environments that drag you down.
9. **Focus on Solutions, Not Just Problems**
   - ○ Instead of dwelling on the issue, ask, "What can I do to improve this?" Alcohol will not improve the situation.
   - ○ Taking action—even small steps—on working to resolve the issue, can help shift your energy from frustration to progress.
10. **Use Affirmations and Positive Self-Talk**
    - ○ Replace negative thoughts with encouraging and empowering statements.
    - ○ Words have power—remind yourself that you are resilient and capable of overcoming challenges.

In your journal, write down and focus on a specific negative situation, and explore how you can turn it around. Also, think about what steps you can take to resolve a negative situation that may arise in the future.

We need to realize that drinking does not solve a negative emotion. Being sober teaches us to confront feelings and emotions head-on. This is how we need to start to resolve negative situations. Not drinking helps us resolve the situation instead of not resolving them by drinking.

Day 26

It can vary from person to person, but a common habit usually takes at least 2 months. In the book *The World's Greatest Salesman* by Og Mandino, they talk about habit and how to transform a person. It's a great book; you can find it in audio-book form as well—I recommend it. Here are the 10 scrolls that they mention in the book, which can also be used for sobriety and becoming a better person overall. I have added how they can help when working to be sober. Along with the affirmations that remain, try to follow these 10 scrolls. In the book, they are to follow each scroll for 30 days. For this exercise **in your journal write down** one and live it for this day. The one that stood out to you write in your journal and write why you chose this scroll to live by today, then—try to live with it for 30 days. Then in 30 days, try a new one. This will help you understand the power of working to create a habit.

The 10 Scrolls and Their Habitual Lessons:

1. **Scroll I – Today I Begin a New Life**
   a. Develop the habit of **renewal** and embracing change. Being sober is a new beginning—remember that. The old you is leaving for a better version of you.
   b. Commit to starting fresh every day, leaving past failures behind. Focus on staying sober for today leaving past thoughts behind.
2. **Scroll II – I Will Greet This Day with Love in My Heart**
   a. Build the habit of **kindness, love, and positive thinking** toward others.
   b. Overcome anger, hate, and negativity by choosing to love in every interaction. This will help you become the person you want to be in sobriety. Treat others the way you want to be treated.

3. **Scroll III – I Will Persist Until I Succeed**
   a. Create the habit of **persistence and resilience** in the face of failure. Commit to telling your mind you don't need alcohol to live today. The more you persist in not drinking, the longer you will stay clean.
   b. Never give up and keep moving forward despite setbacks. You control alcohol, It doesn't control you.

4. **Scroll IV – I Am Nature's Greatest Miracle**
   a. Develop the habit of **self-confidence and self-worth**.
   b. Recognize your uniqueness and potential to achieve greatness. Staying sober will help you achieve greatness in your life.

5. **Scroll V – I Will Live This Day as If It Is My Last**
   a. Cultivate the habit of **living in the present** and making the most of every moment. That means don't turn to booze. Live in the moment today—be sober and happy. One minute at a time.

6. **Scroll VI – Today I Will Be Master of My Emotions**
   a. Build emotional discipline and control your reactions to situations.
   b. Don't let emotions dictate actions—respond wisely instead. When you face a challenge in daily life, choose intelligently and don't turn to alcohol.

7. **Scroll VII – I Will Laugh at the World**

    a. Develop the habit of **maintaining a sense of humor and perspective**.

    b. Don't take life too seriously—learn to find joy and laughter in challenges. Remember, alcohol will cause depression and make you feel like crap later.

8. **Scroll VIII – Today I Will Multiply My Value a Hundredfold**

    a. Focus on **continuous self-improvement** and add value to others.

    b. Always strive to grow and do more than expected. Do some extra meetings when you feel the need. Call a sober friend and go over.

9. **Scroll IX – I Will Act Now**

    a. Build the habit of **acting immediately** rather than waiting.

    b. Avoid the extra thoughts about alcohol—reprogram the thought process to "No, that stuff is crap." Don't overthink—take action now to say no to the booze. Work to chang your thoughts and create a Paradigm shift of thoughts.

10. **Scroll X – I Will Pray for Guidance**

    a. Foster the habit of **seeking wisdom, gratitude, and faith**. Sometimes we need to let go and let God. Prayer does work for many and can help you too.

    b. Trust in a higher purpose and seek guidance in decision-making.

Day 27

Success comes with daily habits over time. Discipline, persistence, and a positive mindset are key factors in staying sober. One of the hardest things when staying sober is continuing to have a positive mindset. You need to start by telling yourself, "I am now working to live my best life." That means if we can understand that we are working to be sober to live our best life, then we are halfway to winning the battle of staying sober for good.

You may have been working to stay sober for 30 days. You can see how far you have come and realize that this is a much better way to live. Drinking and being hungover all the time is not worth it. Spending your weekends sick from a hangover is not the way to live. All the new things you can get done by staying sober are amazing.

In your journal today, write down what you feel it will take to stay away from alcohol long-term, and how you can achieve this. Focus on this today and dig deep. Write it all down in your journal. Map out your personal game plan to stay away from alcohol for good. It's your personal journey and what will it take to completely stop for good?

Day 28

Today we are going to dig deep into the Wheel of Life assessment. While we did some assessment on Day 3, today I want to really focus on the different aspects of your life. Below are the Wheel of Life details to focus on.

In your journal, write down these aspects of your life and break them down.

Wheel of Life Assessment

On a scale from 1 to 10:

- Rate these different aspects of your life from one to ten—1 being the least fulfilled, and 10 being the most fulfilled.
- Career
- Relationships
- Health
- Personal growth
- Spirituality
- Finances
- Fun
- Environment (Your surroundings)

Identify areas that need more balance and focus. If you have a 1 or a 10 in an aspect of your life, can you work to make it closer to a 5? The point of this exercise is to work toward and create balance in your life.

While our career or relationship might be closer to a 10, how can you work to bring the others up (or down) the scale to make it a 5? This will help us understand that while we often put more emphasis on things that are important to us, we sometimes neglect areas that also carry meaning in our lives. We need to work to have more balance in our lives.

Part of stopping for these 30 days is to take a personal inventory of our lives and figure out how we can continue forward without drinking alcohol. We must also realize that alcohol can destroy many aspects of life we live with daily. Creating balance in them will help us stay focused on what's important and how to work and balance our minds.

When we have **balance,** it can create harmony between work, life, and your overall personal well-being.

Day 29

Regulating our emotions.

When we drink, the brain rewires itself to unhealthy habits. If we have been drinking for years, our minds associate alcohol-induced euphoria as rewarding. Yet, you're killing your insides and destroying your mind.

Regulation of our emotions also means you must want to work to control them. Alcohol will not let you do this. These past 29 days, you have been training your mind to solve problems and learning from them each day. We may have failed in our lives, but failure is a part of learning—and now that we have come this far, we are coming to a crossroad.

Small steps are huge victories, and if you've done 29 days with no alcohol, I will say—that is a huge accomplishment! Congratulations.

Will it get easier? Yes, it will! Are there always going to be struggles? Yes. I have given you the tools over the past 29 days to really look inside yourself in multiple ways. You have stepped out of your comfort zone, and we need to keep educating ourselves.

I encourage you to continue the work and get some books from Amazon that deal with alcohol and addiction. You have this one, and there are a few other good ones. Continuing our education and learning everything you can is going to be the key in the next chapter of your life.

We have so many seasons—and now that you have come this far, think of all that you can do with a clear mind on your shoulders. All the things that will come from being sober are a true blessing. **In your Journal today** write down what it means to have a paradigm shift and new mind set. We have worked to establish one way of thinking. It must result in a significant alteration in how you perceive your reality and alcohol. You have the knowledge after these 29 days. Your thoughts have become different. Now apply it as to why you don't ever want to drink again. It as to come from within and put an emotional understanding that this is it. You have come to the cross in the road and can continue the path with no alcohol. Take today to really let all this sink into the subconscious where the decisions are made.

Day 30

The Crossroads.

Here we are—we made it 30 days! You are a true testament to working toward living your best life. So here it is: you have gained so much in the past 30 days. I hope you have been writing in your journal during this time. You now have every tool you need to never go back to drinking again. That's why I call this day *the crossroads.*

You and I both know that alcohol is not our friend, and we shouldn't let it have a seat at our table. We really have two choices at this point: to stay on this path of sobriety or to go back to a miserable life that caused us so much nonsense. Today, I challenge you to keep doing what has worked and stay on this sober path. So many have not made it to 30 days—and here you are: a true sober warrior in the making!

Over these past 30 days, I hope you found what worked for you, and I hope you take it another 30 days. Go for 60! There is an app you can download called *Sober Time*, and it keeps track of how long you've been sober. Just put in the date you started, and it will keep track of the days you have been sober. I look at mine—over a year and a half now while writing this book—and never dreamed I would be getting close to 700 days! Thank God. Honestly, I don't think I would be here to write this book if I had kept drinking.

You must realize all the days you are gaining while being sober!

With all of that said, I will say this: get to meetings, work the 12 steps, and get a sponsor. So many in recovery have sponsors, and it helps them stay sober. It's worth a try. You've made it this far—now give the 12 steps a try. You have already worked on some of the steps just by following this program over the past 30 days. I understand that it's not for everyone and while I do online meetings from time to time. It's not for everyone. Find what works for you and stick to it. This is your journey, and you can make it to whatever works for you. Create the habit for yourself to stay off the alcohol. The longer you stay away the easier it becomes.

Here is what you will gain by staying sober: people around you will look up to you and respect you a lot more. Old friends and family will start coming around—people you may have lost over the years. Your weekends will be so much better without losing all those hours hungover.

The sober journey doesn't end here—it is only just beginning. You have your whole life ahead of you. Stay connected to sober Facebook pages. Seeing others shining—and even seeing those who are struggling—helps us stay focused.

Also, the more you keep your lighthouse windows shining,

the more people will turn to you and ask how you did it. Helping others helps you. Remember that!

I will be the first one to tell you—YOU GOT THIS!

I pray to God that He keeps you on this path of sobriety, and that you help others stop drinking too.

Here's to many years of living your best life. Go have a nice dinner and celebrate your 30 days of NO ALCOHOL! BOOM!!! CONGRATULATIONS! YOU ARE A TESTAMENT TO LIVING YOUR BEST LIFE!

10

THE TRANSITION

In your life, you drank a lot, and you picked up this book to help you stop drinking. This chapter is to consciously reflect and see if you are up for the transition and can stay sober. Here is a breakdown of memories with alcohol:

- I drank for happiness, and it always resulted in making me unhappy.
- I drank for joy, and it made my life miserable.
- I drank for sociability and became argumentative to friends and family.
- I drank for sophistication and became obnoxious.
- I drank for friendship and made enemies.
- I drank for sleep and woke up tired.
- I drank for strength and it only made me weak.
- I drank for relaxation and eventually got the shakes.
- I drank for courage and became uncourageous.
- I drank for confidence and became mentally weak.

- I drank to make conversation when it only slurred my speech.
- I drank to feel heavenly and ended up feeling like hell!

I read this from an unknown author and wanted to make sure to add this. If you drank regularly, you understand all of these quotes. We, as humans, want to find something that can help us escape at times and not become part of its addiction. We are adaptive creations, and when we do things long enough, we adapt to them, and they become us. Undoing something we've done for so long can be so hard to undo. Why is it so hard? Because our minds have learned to enjoy what appears to be exciting, only to become smoke and mirrors. It's a magic trick to the mind. The only way to break free is to work to change your thoughts.

How do you do this? I'll give you an example of how the mind works. If you saw an area of sand and you made the top of the sand smooth with your hand, then run your fingers through the sand, you would have made an impression in the sand with your fingers. That's what happens when you drink alcohol or use mind altering substances, you indent the euphoria into your mind. The only way to take the indentation away is to try to reimpress what has already been stamped. You need to dig deeper than what the alcohol or substance has imprinted and create new imprints. You, as a person, need to find out how you can create those new imprints and wipe the embedded thoughts and beliefs that alcohol has created in our minds.

Most will stop drinking alcohol because they have had a

traumatic event, or their bodies can't take it anymore and it has become a life choice. You either continue to drink and die, or you stop to see how long you can live. We are not promised eternity here on Earth. We want to believe we have forever, but we don't. It's about working to create those new ideas and ideologies of alcohol—and stopping it for good. You spent some time in this book looking for ways to help you stop, and you have just about every tool you will need to create those new imprints in your sand (your mind). We need to build on them and make them crystal clear. This is where you are headed.

The struggles are going to be there, and alcohol is on every corner, in every restaurant, and on every street. It's the most readily available toxic substance available to any human for consumption. There are entire aisles of alcohol in grocery stores. Once we understand that it no longer needs to be in our lives, we need to accept it and find what will work for us to stay away from it.

On the bright side, you will wake up clear-minded and on a new life journey. We can expect things around us to change for the better. The changes that will take place will be something to appreciate, and you won't want to let them go. For me, I decided to never drink again. Why? Because I know if I were to drink, I would only drink more and more and feel like crap again and again. It wasn't working for me anymore. You will accomplish a lot more things than you would if you had been drinking.

"Oh, I drink when I get out of work to relax." I established early in the book it doesn't relax you—it creates more stress mentally and physically. Your mind and body will thank you for stopping drinking, and you are adding days to your life that were taken away by drinking. If you were to walk down a hallway and see all the people suffering from what alcohol did to them, you would never drink again, because you would see the destruction it caused. From dialysis, to having to take pills to stay alive because their liver isn't working. The families it destroyed by the abuse. The mental illness it caused from drinking and depression. It gave so many a stroke and they can't move the left side of their body. The list goes on and on.

You must make a final decision to say, "I don't want that life," and transition to a better, more stable life. That short moment of feeling the euphoria is not worth the long-term effects it will have on your body and your life. If you want to live with those consequences, then continue to drink and see what happens. It won't be fun on that side of the street. It's the undisputed champ in destroying people's lives—time and time again.

The beauty of it is that it's your journey, and that gives it uniqueness and fulfillment. Early in my recovery—or stopping the poison—I wanted to help as many people as I could. I wanted to tell everyone how bad it was and all the things I was seeing and learning. But the reality was, I needed to do it for myself. It would cause more issues with people who didn't see what I was seeing, and they would more than likely not see it. Why? Because they had not hit their rock bottom, or their minds were so far gone from the belief of what alcohol is and does for them. It's a personal accomplishment that no one will experience but you.

It's a great feeling knowing that you are not held down by the shackles of the booze and that you are free at last. There are a lot of people who work hard all day and don't see a problem with having a couple of drinks—and can have a couple of drinks. But for a lot, it's drink to get wasted and feel like crap the next morning. A lot of the bar owners will not care but only want to make a buck and keep their business going. They don't care about your wellbeing. It's not a way to live, and now is the time to make a better life for yourself. Keep your side of the street clean and you will see how others will see that, and realize that your side of the street is a lot better way to live. I keep my lighthouse windows as shiny as I can and let the light out every chance I get—to hopefully one day help those around me see it and stop the poison that is killing them.

There are times in the book where we go over a lot of the same things, but isn't that what alcohol does? We repeat the same things over and over. If you have taken the 30-day alcohol break, you have broken that cycle of "over and over" and are on your way to the top of the hill—ready to go down the hill and listen to your favorite song. Try new songs and start reprogramming your mind.

"It works if you work it" is a quote from Alcoholics Anonymous (AA). It means that if you put in the effort, you can make progress. The full quote is, "It works if you work it— and you're worth it".

The journey of this book will have brought you to many different ideologies and facts about drinking. We have faced our thoughts head on and have a different understanding of what it means to live alcohol-free. Be the change on this planet and know that no one can force you to want to do it. I pray that with all of this; you will find the courage to change your life for good. Read the book several times, find new books, educate yourself, and see the change happen. Pray often and work on building some faith toward a better life!

We only have one life to live. May your days be filled with peace, love, and joy to all. There is only one way to live—and that's sober. I faced The Hard Truth of Stopping Alcohol, and I won! You can too!

Chris Najera

IN CONCLUSION

There is a foundation in this book to really learn about alcohol, know about alcohol, and guide you to work and stop alcohol. The fact is, for many, it's not easy, and you can feel like you are on autopilot, driving to the liquor store when you don't even want to drink. A lot of people will think they are missing out on having fun and that drinking is a good time. You need to realize that it's only destroying you. While it is socially accept-able, most people I have talked to don't even know that it kills 3 million people annually worldwide. It has become one of the most destructive substances on the plant to date. In 4 years, it will have killed 12 million people. That is something to stay the hell away from.

When you start learning that it's killing your insides and causing you problems, we need to look at it in a different light. If you have written in your journal during your 30-day alcohol break that I created, you will have everything you need to completely stop for good. Your mind, body, family and friends will appreciate you and who you become. Not only that, but you will also have a chance to help others who may need the help.

There are two sides to every coin, and the grass is always greener on one side of the street. You can make those final decisions and stick to a better life or go back to a long, destructive life that satisfies nothing. Like the late comedian Freddy Soto said, "You got to know where you came from to know where you're going, bro." So stands true in sobriety—"Regardless."

One life to live, one life given. We only have the rest of our lives to go! Make it your best one! Godspeed! I pray that every one of you make it in sobriety and feels the relief and clear mind it has given me. Life is amazing on this side of the fence!

One day at a time—and it works if you work it!

In memory of all the friends we have lost to alcohol addiction, and the ones who won't want to see the light and live your life to the fullest, Sober AF—I pray for you!

My sober date: 7/26/23
Thank you for reading,
Chris Najera

BIBLIOGRAPHY

Chapter 2 – ChatGPT was used for information on alcohol—how alcohol works on a neurological level.

All references to alcohol-related deaths, city totals, and numbers were researched through ChatGPT.

Chapter 3 – Mentions of alcohol's hidden agenda and the destruction it causes to the human body were researched through ChatGPT.

Chapter 4 – Vig Adams, founder of the Facebook group *Alcohol Is Not My Problem Anymore*, shared 13 steps that I found most beneficial in facilitating my own recovery.

In chapter 7 – I quoted Og Mandino, *The World's Greatest Salesman*, and used the 10 scrolls with a twist to address addiction and alcohol.

Chapter 8 – I mention Charles Nieman and his book *Endings and New Beginnings*.

Chapter 9 – Mentions of Alcoholic Anonymous and its 12 steps.

ACKNOWLEDGMENTS

This book would not exist without the love, support, and unwavering belief of the people who stood by me during the darkest chapters of my life and walked beside me on the road to recovery.

To my mother, Pat Hodgkins—putting everyone first before yourself, your compassion, and endless understanding helped me accomplish this book of hope. Even when I was lost in addiction, you cared unconditionally. You showed me what it means to keep faith alive, even in the face of hopelessness. I owe so much of my healing to the foundation you gave me, while always helping where I couldn't.

To my fiancée, Jaymie Vasquez—you were not only my partner in life, but a true partner in my sobriety. Your courage, understanding, and tireless commitment helped pave the way to a future I once thought impossible. Thank you for standing beside me when I couldn't stand on my own, and for believing in me when I didn't believe in myself. I will be forever thankful for what you did for me in my darkest hours, struggling through my addiction, your love never wavered.

ABOUT THE AUTHOR

Christopher J. Najera is a recovering alcoholic who has transformed personal struggle into a story of strength, redemption, and hope. After battling alcohol addiction for over 34 years, barely making it out alive, embarked on a transformative journey of recovery. With raw honesty and emotional depth, Chris shares the perils of hitting rock bottom, what happens when your mind gets hijacked by alcohol, sober struggles, and the haunting isolation that addiction breeds, also uncovering the pivotal turning points and what it takes to embrace sobriety. Through aha moments of revelation, shame and self-forgiveness, Chris came to understand that recovery is not a single event, but a lifelong process fueled by courage, community, and unwavering self-reflection. In this powerful debut, Chris Najera not only recounts his own experiences but also offers insight into the emotional and psychological toll of addiction, the stigma surrounding it, and the small yet monumental victories that define each day of sobriety. Now getting close to 2 years sober, Chris completed his life coach certification as well as several studies for recovery, is an advocate for addiction awareness and mental health, speaking publicly and working with others to break the silence around alcohol use disorders. His story is a testament to resilience, showing that even in the darkest moments, there is always the possibility of light—and that healing is possible for anyone willing to seek it. You got this, and you can do this!

Sober date: 7/26/2023

JOURNAL WRITING OR NOTES